IN LIGHT OF
ETERNITY

IN LIGHT OF ETERNITY

Perspectives on Heaven

RANDY ALCORN

WATERBROOK
PRESS

IN LIGHT OF ETERNITY
PUBLISHED BY WATERBROOK PRESS
5446 North Academy Boulevard, Suite 200
Colorado Springs, Colorado 80918
A division of Random House, Inc.

All Scripture quotations, unless otherwise noted, are taken from the *Holy Bible, New International Version®*. NIV®. Copyright© 1973, 1978, 1984 by International Bible Society. Used by permission of Zondervan Publishing House. All rights reserved. Scripture quotations marked (KJV) are from the *King James Version* of the Bible. Any italics in Scripture quotes are the author's.

Portions of this work were originally published in: *Edge of Eternity* by Randy Alcorn, copyright 1998 by Eternal Perspective Ministries, published by WaterBrook Press. *Deadline* by Randy Alcorn, copyright 1994 by Randy Alcorn. Used by permission of Multnomah Publishers, Inc. *Dominion* by Randy Alcorn, copyright 1996 by Randy Alcorn. Used by permission of Multnomah Publishers, Inc. Some concepts in this book are adapted from *Money, Possessions and Eternity* by Randy Alcorn (Wheaton, Illinois: Tyndale House, 1989).

The A. W. Tozer quotes on page 6 and page 147 are from *Of God and Men* (Harrisburg, Pennsylvania: Christian Publications, 1960), pages 129–130. The Tozer quote on page 160 is from *Born After Midnight* (Harrisburg, Pennsylvania: Christian Publications, Inc., 1959), page 107.

The C. S. Lewis selections on page 128 and page 139 are from *The Weight of Glory* (New York: Macmillan, 1949), pages 18–19 and 3–4. The *Chronicles of Narnia* passages on pages 32, 33, 81, and 152 are from Lewis's *The Last Battle* (New York: Macmillan, 1956), pages 183–184 and 180. The Lewis quotes on pages 143, 144–145, and 163–164 are from *Mere Christianity* (New York: Macmillan, 1960), pages 120 and 188. The quotes on pages 157 and 158 are from Lewis's *The Problem of Pain* (New York: Macmillan, 1948), pages 115, 145, and 147.

ISBN 1-57856-299-6

Printed in the United States of America
1999—First Edition

10 9 8 7 6 5 4 3 2 1

To my trusted friend and brother Barry Arnold
&
to all those who've given their lives to the high calling of world missions, becoming less at home on earth in light of their true home in heaven
&
to Mom and Dad, my friend Jerry Hardin, and many other loved ones who've made it home before me—
I can hardly wait to see you again.

Contents

Acknowledgments

Thanks to Thomas Womack and Doug Gabbert for suggesting we assemble my articles on heaven and eternal rewards as the beginning point for this book. Thanks especially to Thomas for looking through my writings and organizing them, allowing me to add and edit more efficiently. Thanks to Laura Barker for all her detailed work on the final product. Thanks also to Dan Rich, Rebecca Price, Lisa Bergren, Steve Cobb, and others at Water-Brook. I deeply appreciate all your efforts.

Thanks to my wonderful wife and best friend, Nanci—I can't say enough about who you are and all you do. You're God's gift to me. And to my terrific daughters, Angela and Karina, for always being so encouraging and delightful and for making parenting a pleasure. Karina, thanks also for your skillful help in editing the first manuscript. Thanks to Angela Alcorn, Janie Stump, and Sarah Thebarge for checking Scripture references.

Thanks to Bonnie Hiestand and Kathy Norquist for everything from typing to assistance with phone calls and e-mail, but especially for your faithful service to our King and to EPM.

Thanks to C. J. Mahaney and Dave Harvey—and other dear friends in PDI churches—who encouraged me to write some more nonfiction.

On heaven, I've benefited from the writings and teachings of many, including John Bunyan, Joseph Bayly, Peter Kreeft, John Gilmore, Joni Eareckson Tada, John MacArthur, and Gerry Breshears. On reward, Bruce Wilkinson and Erwin Lutzer. On our longing for God, C. S. Lewis, A. W. Tozer, and John Piper.

Thanks to my brothers and sisters at Good Shepherd Community Church, as well as the faithful supporters of Eternal Perspective Ministries. Your assistance—and above all your prayers—do not go unnoticed. You'll play a major part in touching the hearts of those who read this book.

The highest praise goes to the person who made me and for whom I was made: the Carpenter from Nazareth, King Jesus. My heartfelt thanks to you for your heart-piercing grace and your inexplicable desire to spend eternity with me and others like me. Despite my utter unworthiness, I offer you my heartfelt praise for going to prepare a place for me and for working to prepare me for that place. I love you.

Our prayer, sovereign Lord: that you would use this book to do a miracle of grace. Break through the lies of the evil ones who incessantly try to malign and minimize the glorious nature of our home in heaven. Use these feeble words to point readers to your Word, which alone is grain, not straw, which alone is the rock and fire that man's words—and those of the spirits of darkness—cannot stand up to.

"When I Think About Heaven…"

I once heard a pastor make a startling confession: "Whenever I think about heaven, it makes me depressed. I'd rather just cease to exist when I die."

I tried not to show my shock as I asked him, "Why?"

"I can't stand the thought of that endless tedium. To float around in the clouds with nothing to do but strum a harp…it's all so terribly boring. Heaven doesn't sound much better than hell. I'd rather be annihilated than spend eternity in a place like that."

Where did this Bible-believing, seminary-educated pastor get such an idea of heaven? Certainly not from Scripture, where Paul said to depart and be with Christ was "better by far" than staying on earth (Philippians 1:23). And yet, though my friend was more honest about it than most, I've found many Christians share the same misconceptions about heaven.

I've received thousands of letters concerning heaven because I picture it in my novels. Here's a letter that came last week:

I've been a Christian since I was five. I'm married to a youth pastor. The reason I am writing is to thank you for writing *Deadline*.

When I was seven, a teacher at my Christian school told me that when I got to heaven I wouldn't know anyone or anything from earth. I was terrified of dying. I was never told any different by anyone either.

Until reading *Deadline* I was still terrified of heaven. But I'm not afraid anymore. Heaven will be great.

It's been really hard for me to advance in my Christian walk because of this fear of heaven. You don't know the weight that's been lifted off me. I cried every time I read about Finney being in heaven and all his experiences. Now I can't wait to get there.

Because of pervasive distortions of what heaven is like, it's common for Christians not to look forward to heaven—or even to dread it. I think there's only one explanation for how these appalling viewpoints have gripped so many of God's people: Satan. Demonic deception.

Jesus said of the devil, "When he lies, he speaks his native language, for he is a liar and the father of lies" (John 8:44). Some of Satan's favorite lies are about heaven. Revelation 13:6 tells us the satanic beast "opened his mouth to blaspheme God, and to slander his name and his dwelling place and those who live in heaven." Our enemy slanders three things: God's person, God's people, and God's place—heaven.

After being forcibly evicted from heaven (Isaiah 14:12-15),

the devil is bitter not only toward God, but toward us and the place that's no longer his. (It must be maddening for Satan to realize we're now entitled to the home he was kicked out of.) What better way for demons to attack than to whisper lies about the very place God tells us to set our hearts and minds on (Colossians 3:1-2)?

Paul warned us to be aware of the devil's schemes (2 Corinthians 2:11) and put on God's armor to stand against them (Ephesians 6:11). Make no mistake—one of Satan's favorite tactics is feeding us an unworthy, dull, and distorted view of heaven. He knows we'll lack motivation to tell others about Jesus when our view of heaven isn't that much better than our concept of hell.

Look at all those people walking the streets, working in offices, standing in lines, sitting in restaurants. Their eyes are filled with needs, hopes, longings. The world tells them they're just molecules and DNA, time plus chance. But God has "set eternity in the hearts of men" (Ecclesiastes 3:11). Their hearts cry out for eternal realities, for what will last, what really matters.

They search for something, *anything,* to fill the raging emptiness within. Satan offers them anesthetics that temporarily dull the pain, but the anesthetics wear off. The promise of fulfillment is always broken. So they go right on searching in all the wrong places. They turn to drugs, sex, money, and power for the same reason they turn to religion and self-help seminars. Their instincts tell them "something's missing, there has to be more."

And they're absolutely right. Something *is* missing.

The first thing missing is the person we were made for—Jesus. Haggai 2:7 refers to Messiah as "the desired of all nations," the one all people of all cultures long for.

3

But there's something else missing. Every human heart yearns for not only a person but a place. The place we were made for. The place made for us.

In Revelation 3:12, Jesus makes a great promise to those who obey him: "I will write on him the name of my God and the name of the city of my God, the new Jerusalem, which is coming down out of heaven from my God; and I will also write on him my new name." Jesus says he will put on us the name of the person *and* the name of the place (heaven) for which we were made.

Jesus used the phrases "kingdom of God" and "kingdom of heaven" interchangeably (Matthew 19:23-24). God's person and God's place are that closely connected (Luke 15:18).

We spend our lives longing for this person and this place. Just as people restlessly move from relationship to relationship seeking the person they were made for, they move from location to location seeking the place they were made for. Somewhere new and better. A bigger house. A different city. The suburbs. A new neighborhood—safer, nicer, with better schools. That dream house in the country. That idyllic mountain chalet. That perfect beach cottage.

Think about it—we have the very answers the world is crying out for, yet our wrong views of God's person and God's place silence and distort our message. What a triumph for Satan that we would actually pass on to our churches, our children, and our world a dreary view of heaven—and by implication a dreary view of God.

When Jesus said to us, "I am going there [to heaven] to prepare a place for you.... I will come back and take you to be with me that you also may be where I am" (John 14:2-3), he spoke as a groom to his bride-to-be. These are words of love and romance. How would any bride who loves her husband-to-be respond to them? She'd be thrilled. Not a single day would go by, not a single *hour*, in which the bride wouldn't anticipate joining her beloved in that place he prepared for her to live with him forever.

Like a bride's dreams of sharing a home with her groom, our love for heaven should be overflowing and contagious, just as our love for God should be (Revelation 19:7). Our passion for God and our passion for heaven should be inseparable. The more I learn about God, the more excited I get about heaven. The more I learn about heaven, the more excited I get about God.

How it must wound the heart of our bridegroom to see us clinging to this roach-infested hovel called earth, dreading the thought of leaving it, when he has hand-built a magnificent estate for us, a place beautiful and wondrous beyond measure.

What's your attitude toward heaven, your theology of heaven? Does it fill you with joy and excitement? How much thought do you give to heaven? How often do you and your church and your family talk about it?

If you lack a passion for heaven, I can almost guarantee it's because you have a weak, deficient, and distorted theology of heaven. (Or you're making choices that conflict with heaven's agenda.) A robust, accurate, and biblically energized view of heaven will bring you a new spiritual passion.

Our problem isn't that we lack passion in general. We all have it—look at the way we stand up and cheer at sporting events. (Nanci and I do anyway.) The problem is that we get most passionate about things that don't ultimately matter—the perfect season, the perfect house, the perfect lawn, the perfect car. None of these is bad—notice I didn't list pornography, adultery, fornication, theft, and hatred. Our problem is that the good things fueling our passion are only secondary, while we lack passion for what's primary. To derail us, all Satan needs to do is minimize our passion for two things—the person of God and the place of God.

A. W. Tozer said,

> Let no one apologize for the powerful emphasis Christianity lays upon the doctrine of the world to come. Right there lies its immense superiority to everything else within the whole sphere of human thought or experience.... We do well to think of the long tomorrow.

The greatest weakness of the western church today is arguably our failure to think of the long tomorrow—to take seriously the reality that heaven is our home. Out of this springs our love affair with this world and our failure to live now in light of eternity.

When my family goes on a trip, we like to know in advance something about where we're going. If we're planning a vacation, we study the brochures and maps to know the destination's attractions. But we don't want to know everything—we do like surprises.

So think of this book as belonging in the bookstore's travel section. It's sort of a travel guide to heaven. And if you want your children or grandchildren to be more excited about heaven than the Grand Canyon or Disney World or summer camp, open up the Bible and talk to them about heaven's attractions, not just earth's.

Home

How acquainted are you with the final destination of the road you're traveling?

In my novel *Edge of Eternity*, Nick Seagrave—who wakes up in another world—chooses many wrong paths before he finally joins with others to follow the red road. It leads him to a great chasm. After he's carried over it by the mysterious Chasm-crosser, the road resumes on the other side. Occasionally Nick catches sight of his destination:

> I turned in the darkness and beheld Charis, the glowing City of Light. The joy of that place was like a volcanic explosion, spectacular and thrilling, never subsiding. I could feel it from here.
>
> "I see…my home."
>
> I laughed aloud. All my life I'd been going out, a wanderer without a home. Now I was coming in, a traveler headed home. I considered the joyous irony—the places I'd always been were never my home. And my true home was a place I'd never been.

Have you ever thought about that? The Bible teaches that for Christians, our home is where Christ is, in heaven (2 Corinthians 5:8). Our home is a place we've never been.

When we arrive there, heaven will immediately feel like home because we'll instinctively connect it to all we longed for and occasionally caught magical glimpses of while on earth. But in heaven we won't just look back; we'll look forward to and anticipate all that's ahead of us there. The longer we're in heaven, the more memories we'll make and the more our home will be...home. It won't lose its homeyness—it will always gain more.

When the Bible tells us heaven is our home, what meaning should we attach to the word? I can visit somewhere and say, "This feels like home." I'm saying it reminds me of home and has some of the qualities of home. But what are those qualities?

Familiarity is one—a fond familiarity. I was raised in a non-Christian home, but I have countless pleasurable memories from childhood. When I ride my bike through my old neighborhood (only a few miles away), that fond familiarity comes over me like a wave. The hills, the houses, the fences and fields, the schoolyard where I played football and shot hoops.

I find myself gazing at the house I grew up in. Every room in that house, every inch of that property reverberates with memories of my father, mother, brother, and friends, as well as dogs and cats and frogs and lizards. When I go to my childhood home, I step back into a place inseparable from who I was and am, inseparable from my family and friends.

That's a central quality of home: It's a place with loved ones. The "homeness" of the house I live in now is inseparable from my wife, Nanci, and my daughters, Angela and Karina. Memories of extended family and friends who've stayed with us also contribute to the homeness of this place. Everything here speaks of time spent with one another: playing together, talking together, eating together, reading together, crying together, praying together, charting the course of our lives together. Home is where you're with the ones you love.

The best part of heaven is that we'll be with our bridegroom, Jesus. Second best? We'll be with our family and friends who know God. That's why, when Christian loved ones die, God tells us not to grieve like those who have no hope, but to comfort and encourage each other by anticipating the ultimate family reunion (1 Thessalonians 4:13-18). That's why heaven should mean more to us every time a friend moves there.

In heaven we'll be at home with our Christian ancestors and, eventually, our descendants.

Home is a place where you fit right in. It's the place you were made for. Most houses we live in on earth weren't really made just for us. But heaven is.

I love to go snorkeling and watch those multicolored fish in their natural environment. Occasionally I see ocean fish in an aquarium. I enjoy watching them, but I always feel like something's wrong. They don't belong there. It's not their home. They weren't made for a little glass box. They were made for a great ocean. I suppose the fish don't know any better, but I wonder if their instincts tell them their true home is elsewhere, they were made for another place. I know our instincts tell us this world isn't our home, that we were made for someplace bigger and better.

Home is also about comfort. It's a place you can take off the dress clothes and put on jeans and a sweatshirt and throw yourself down on the couch and relax. It's a refuge from the world. It's a place you *want* to be. I've traveled to many countries and as much as I enjoy them, I always love to come home. That craving for home is sweet and deep. Home is our reference point, what we always come back to. No matter how much we enjoy our adventures away, we look forward to coming home.

Home is where friends come to visit us. Home is where we read and reflect and listen to music we enjoy. It's where we putter and plant gardens and rest to gain strength for our tasks. Home is the place I inhale the wonderful aroma of strong rich coffee every morning. (Okay, you hate coffee? Your loss.) Home is where Nanci fixes wonderful meals, including the world's best apple pie.

Eating, talking, and laughing together make a house a home. In heaven we'll have feasts together (Matthew 8:11). In fact, "the LORD Almighty will prepare a feast of rich food for all peoples…the best of meats and the finest of wines" (Isaiah 25:6). Considering who's doing the cooking, how good do you think *that* meal will be?

Jesus said we who weep now on earth will laugh in heaven (Luke 6:21). We'll be childlike there (Matthew 19:14). Who laughs more than children? When you think of heaven, think of delighted, infectious laughter with those you love. Get ready to hear the laughter of God, who made us in his image, with the capacity to laugh.

I realize it sounds like I'm romanticizing home. Many people, it's true, have had bad experiences in their earthly homes. But the point is, our home in heaven is our real home. It will have all the good things about our earthly home, multiplied many times, but none of the bad.

"Delight yourself in the LORD and he will give you the desires of your heart" (Psalm 37:4). God invites us to be delighted in him, his place, his plan, his people. Home is the place where delight in a cherished Father or beloved bridegroom flourishes. Home is a fountainhead of delight. Home is where you enjoy the most enchanting moments.

The world has a saying—"You can never go home again." It means that while you were gone, home changed and so did you. In fact, your old house may have been destroyed or sold. It may be forever inaccessible to you.

In contrast, when this life is over, God's children *will* be able to come home…for the very first time. And because that home— unlike our houses on earth—will never burn or be flooded or blown away, we'll never have to wonder whether home will still be there when we return. Heaven will never disappear and never lose the magic of home.

For years I've had taped to my computer a prayer reminder for homeless children, sent to me by Action International, an outstanding missions organization. It cites Lamentations 2:11-19, crying out for the hungry children in the streets. There are more than one hundred million street children in the world today, in desperate need of an earthly home, Christ, and the hope of a home in heaven. Who will appreciate heaven more than those who have been homeless on earth?

If heaven is truly our home, then it must have these qualities we associate with home. *Home* as a term for heaven is not simply a metaphor. It describes an actual, physical place—a place built by our bridegroom, a place we'll share with loved ones, a place of fond familiarity and comfort and refuge, a place of marvelous smells and tastes, fine food and great conversation, of contemplation and interaction and expressing the gifts and passions God has given us. It will also be a place of unprecedented freedom and adventure. (More about that later.)

I read a statement by an evangelical theologian who says heaven is "more a state of mind than a place." But what does this mean? In the Bible heaven is not simply an attitude or positive thinking or imagining the best. Of course, contemplating heaven should affect our attitude. But that's very different than saying heaven is a state of mind. On the contrary, heaven is a real physical place. And whenever we're thinking accurately, it will be our reference point for all other places.

Jesus said, "I go to prepare a *place* for you" (John 14:2, KJV). He didn't say, "I go to an indescribable realm devoid of physical properties, where your disembodied spirit will float around, and which is nothing at all like what you've ever thought of as home."

If that were the case, he might just as well have said nothing. But he didn't say nothing—he said *something.* He told us of an actual place he was preparing. He also told us why—"And if I go and prepare a place for you, I will come back and take you to be with me *that you also may be where I am*" (John 14:2-3).

Home, Jesus knew, is where you're with the people you love the most in the place you love the most. And, incredibly, the longing of the Carpenter-King—he who holds the title deed to heaven—is that we should join him as his beloved bride and live with him there forever.

"The LORD will take delight in you.… As a bridegroom rejoices over his bride, so will your God rejoice over you" (Isaiah 62:4-5).

Now think about *that* for a few million years!

A Smile of Understanding

When the queen of Sheba finally came to Solomon's kingdom and beheld its glory, she exclaimed, "I did not believe what they said until I came and saw with my own eyes" (2 Chronicles 9:6). But she was most impressed with Solomon himself. She said to him, "not even half the greatness of your wisdom was told me; you have far exceeded the report I heard."

How much more will heaven transcend our expectations? How much more will we be impressed with the greatness of God when at last we see him face to face? To say the least, he will far exceed all we've heard about him.

"The city does not need the sun or the moon to shine on it, for the glory of God gives it light, and the Lamb is its lamp" (Revelation 21:23). Christ himself will illuminate all heaven. He will be heaven's center of gravity. "Let us fix our eyes on Jesus" (Hebrews 12:2). We don't have to wait until heaven to fix our eyes on him. We can get a head start now on gaining the eternal perspective we'll all one day have.

Do you have a life's verse? Mine is 2 Corinthians 4:18. It's on our ministry stationery, on our web page, and at the end of every e-mail I send:

"We fix our eyes not on what is seen, but on what is unseen. For what is seen is temporary, but what is unseen is eternal."

That wasn't always my favorite verse. It grew on me over many years, through some difficult losses.

Eighteen years ago my mother, who was also one of my closest friends, died of cancer. That night Nanci and I wrote letters to our oldest daughter, Karina, who was then only two and a half.

Nanci wrote this:

Dear Karina,

About twenty minutes ago, your Grandma Alcorn died. Daddy is now over at their house with Grandpa and Lance.

I'm writing this to you, because Grandma loved you so much. Her joy was never more complete than when you were around—even in her last days here on earth when she was in pain.

I believe the thing she enjoyed doing most with you was lying on her bed and reading you Bible stories. I know that her prayers for you, Karina, were that you would grow to love Jesus as much as she did.

I loved your Grandma; I'll miss her greatly. But the thing that saddens me most is the loss you and baby Angela have in the passing of a wonderful grandmother. She wanted to take you on long trips to the beach someday. She would have contributed so much to your spiritual life.

But our Lord knows best. His timing is perfect. Grandma Alcorn is in his presence now. You've often said during her final illness, "When Jesus comes to take Grandma to heaven, she will be able to walk again!"

Just tonight, when I was through praying with you in bed, you asked, "When Grandma Alcorn dies, and Jesus takes her to heaven, will he take her bed with her?"

I said, "No, honey, she won't need a bed in heaven."

"But I mean her hospital bed," you said.

I told you no, that she wouldn't need her hospital bed in heaven.

Then you said, "She won't need her hospital bed in heaven because she can lay in Jesus' lap!"

Praise the Lord, Grandma Alcorn is in Jesus' lap right now!

Love,
Mom

When I got home a few hours later I wrote this:

My dearest Karina,

I've just read your mother's letter to you about Grandma Alcorn. It's now 3:30 A.M., a funny time to be writing you. But I've been home from Grandpa's just a little while.

As soon as I came home, about 3:00, I went right to

your bedroom to wake you up. I thought you should know Grandma had died. You were *so* tired, and your eyes kept rolling back as I sat you up in my lap. Finally I knew you were awake, and I asked you, "Karina, do you know where Grandma Alcorn is right now?"

I was sure the answer would be "no." Or maybe you'd say "in bed" since Grandma has been on her sickbed several months. But immediately, without any hesitation, you smiled and said, "Yes, Daddy—she's in heaven."

A wave of electricity went through me. You knew with absolute certainty. There wasn't a hesitation or a doubt. Maybe Jesus whispered it to you in your sleep. Perhaps he let Grandma send a special message to you from heaven. But in any case, you knew exactly where Grandma was.

For several minutes I hugged you tight on your bed and cried very hard. Everything your mom said in her letter about Grandma was true. You always had the most special times when you were with her.

I, too, ache because you had so little time together. Yet I marvel at how close you were in that time. If Grandma sees you as you grow up (I suspect the Lord will let her), she will be so proud. More than anything she would want you to love Jesus with all your heart and to serve him always.

Karina, you are God's gift to me. I love you and your baby sister more than any father has ever loved his daughters. I pray that you and Angela will grow up to be as wonderful as your mom and your grandma.

As I write these things, tears are flowing down my face. How thankful I am to our loving God for giving me such a special family.

I love you, sweetheart.

Daddy

I'll never forget the smile on Karina's face at 3:00 A.M. that dark night when I woke her up to give her what you'd think would have been devastating news. But Karina immediately and accurately grasped something few people do—that she had every reason to be happy for her grandmother. She was not smiling because she didn't understand. She was smiling precisely because she *did* understand.

She knew her grandmother was with the Person she was made for in the place she was made for. Karina literally believed— not just in her head but in her heart—everything we'd told her about heaven.

Though she would miss her grandmother greatly, she understood that this wasn't the end of their relationship, but only an interruption. She knew her grandmother was in heaven and that she would one day join her there. Her theology of heaven was rock-solid.

How does this two-and-a-half-year-old's understanding compare with yours? Do you want to deepen that understanding in your heart as well as in your mind? If so, read on.

Three

So Much
to Think About

The death-row prisoner wrote, "Being at home with God and his angels…that's a lot to think about."

Yes, it is—for all of us.

In the Midwest lives a woman who two decades ago was looking for a way to reach out. She made contact with a death-row prison ministry and began writing to a man named Durlyn who'd been convicted of horrible crimes.

For years she witnessed to this man, but she did not meet him until sixteen years went by and Durlyn's execution was scheduled—for November 19, 1997. She felt it was time for her and her husband to make the ten-hour drive to meet him.

Their visit was powerful. Durlyn told them that when he first received her letters, he was determined to remain a hardened criminal. But God used her diligence and love, along with other Christians he brought into his life, to soften Durlyn's heart and draw him to a saving knowledge of Jesus Christ.

She'd sent him a copy of my novel *Dominion.* In his thank-you letter to her he'd written, "Once it gets to the part about the Lord and heaven and what all takes place, your mind just opens up. Being at home with God and his angels, that's a lot to think about."

Durlyn told her he had stopped reading *Dominion* when he got to the part about God showing one of the characters around heaven and saying, "This is all yours." Durlyn wanted to save this last part of the book to read the day before he was executed. In so many ways, he said, the book seemed to have been written just for him.

After the woman's visit with Durlyn, she contacted me to ask if I would write him a letter. This is what I wrote:

Dear Durlyn,

I'm glad our Lord has spoken to you through *Dominion,* and above all I'm delighted you've come to know Jesus.

None of us deserves God's grace—if we deserved it, we wouldn't need it. Despite our complete unworthiness, he offers us the gift of eternal life based on his death for our sins on the cross. It's an awesome thing to realize God has seen us at our worst and still loves us.

No matter what sins we've committed, Durlyn, I know that if we've both repented and accepted Christ's gift of eternal life, we are brothers and will see each other again on the other side. I look forward to meeting you there.

I have a request for you. My mother, a devoted follower of Christ, died sixteen years ago. My father was very hostile to the gospel. After years of saying "no" to God, he accepted Christ as his Savior five years ago, at the age of eighty-four. Dad died in February, at age eighty-nine, and my family and I were with him when he made the exodus from this world to the next. In fact, Dad's birthday—his ninetieth—is November 19.

So, Durlyn, since you're scheduled to die that day, I'd like to ask you to give my Mom and Dad a hug for me and say "happy birthday" to Dad. I suspect they're seeing a lot of what's going on here, but please tell them I love them and can't wait to see them again.

And when you talk with our Lord, even though he knows this and everything else, tell him how much I love him and how much I look forward to seeing him face to face. I tell him that myself, but if you wouldn't mind passing on the message, I'd appreciate it.

I've marked my calendar and will be praying for you between now and the 19th. I look forward to meeting you, brother. It won't be long before we're both living in the world for which we were made.

Your friend,
Randy Alcorn

Yes, Durlyn, you were right—for those of us still waiting to join you there, our future in heaven offers so much to think about. How thankful I am to God for what he's already revealed to us about it.

Four

Just Wishful Thinking?

In *Dominion,* the novel Durlyn read on death row, the following scene occurs the moment a character dies:

> Dani Rawls awoke again, this time not to a scene of agonized confusion but to a glowing quiet passageway. Behind her lay a land of shadows, a gray and colorless two-dimensional flatland. Ahead of her lay something that defied description...a fresh and utterly captivating place, resonating with color and beauty.
>
> She could not only see and hear it, but feel and smell and taste it, even from a distance. The light beckoned her to come dive into it with abandon, as cool water beckons on a blistering August afternoon.
>
> Already everything within her told her this was the Place that defined all places, the Place by which all places must be judged. It reached out to Dani, playfully grabbing at her, drawing her soul as a powerful magnet draws iron filings.
>
> "The colors. So many colors!" In comparison to this, all the colors of earth she'd enjoyed so much had been no

more than shades of gray. Now there was an infinite rainbow of colors, reaching as far beyond earth's rainbow as sunlight beyond a match flame.

"I'm getting stronger. I can feel it."

Only moments ago she'd been so weary, bone tired, the way she'd felt many nights caring for her sick children, alone without a husband.... How was she moving so quickly while still feeling too drained to move?

Wait. She was being carried. Carried in giant arms. How could she not have realized it until now?

She turned her head and looked up at a sculptured face. Who was this?

She stared at his arms, brawny and strong. The muscles were taut but not bulging, suggesting he wasn't taxed by her weight, that she was a light burden or that he was used to bearing heavy ones. Maybe like her slave forefathers. She was thankful for his strength and felt her own body infusing with energy.

She remembered her Bible. Lazarus was carried to heaven by angels. Was this an angel sent to carry her home? A slightly unnatural grin broke across his marbly face. "Hello, Dani."

"Who are you?" she asked. "An angel sent to get me?"

"Not sent to get you. Beckoned to take you. I've been with you all along. We're both going home."

"Home? You mean…home, like in the Bible?"

"Just like in the Bible."

"I didn't hear a trumpet sound."

"The trumpet comes later, at the return and the resurrection. This is not that day. This is the day of your exodus from mortality to life."

After reading my novels, people often tell me, "These pictures of heaven are exciting and they ring true. But are they based on Scripture?"

The answer, for the most part, is yes. The information Scripture provides us about the world to come is substantial, with enough detail to help us envision it, but not so much to make us think we can fully comprehend it. I believe God expects us to recognize the limits and flaws of our imaginations, but to utilize them nonetheless (remembering always that though we're using our imaginations, heaven is more real than anything we've ever seen or touched). If God didn't want us to imagine what heaven will be like, he wouldn't have told us what he has.

But a caution is necessary. Bookstores are burgeoning with accounts of after-death experiences and interactions with angelic beings. Many of these are unbiblical and misleading, full of false doctrine. They imply that those who don't know Christ will be welcomed into heaven, contrary to John 14:6, Acts 4:12, and many other passages. Just because someone thinks he saw Jesus or an angel in a near-death experience doesn't mean it's true. Scripture warns us that "Satan himself masquerades as an angel of light" (2 Corinthians 11:14).

If those who believe the Scriptures fail to reverently exercise our God-given imaginations where the Bible opens the door for us to do so, we will leave portrayals of the afterlife in the hands of those unconcerned with fidelity to God's Word.

I've studied and taught about heaven and eternal rewards for many years. In my stories, I've taken biblically revealed truths and developed (hopefully not distorted) them in a speculative (hopefully not reckless) fashion. I've sought to include only concepts and portrayals which conform to, or at least do not violate, biblical teaching.

While the experience that awaits us will inevitably prove many of my depictions inaccurate in the details and all of them woefully incomplete, I've sought to fuel and govern my imagination by the Scriptures, many of which I cite in this book. Of course, the reader's mind and imagination should always be submitted to the Word of God as its sole and final authority. You should therefore not trust my opinions or anyone else's, but go to the Scriptures to determine what is true (Acts 17:11).

What Scriptures do I base my ideas on? This book is largely an answer to that question.

Imagine a set of twins having a discussion in their mother's womb:

"You know," one says, "there's a whole world out there—grassy meadows and snowy mountains, splashing streams and waterfalls, horses and dogs and cats and whales and giraffes. There are skyscrapers and cities and people like us—only much bigger—playing games like football and baseball and volleyball and going to the beach."

"Are you crazy?" the other twin responds. "That's just wishful thinking. Everybody knows there's no life after birth."

So it may seem about life after death. You may have a hard time imagining it's real. When you've only been here, here is all you know.

Suppose we traveled to the tundra of the far north and talked with isolated natives who lived most of the year in ice and snow, in a land where stunted shrubs were the largest vegetation. Now imagine telling these people about the tropics—dense green forests, warm sandy beaches lined with palm trees, coconuts and bananas and oranges and dozens of other fruits. Would your hearers understand? Without the necessary reference points, how could they?

Reality isn't restricted by the limits of our ability to understand. Life outside the womb is real though the child cannot imagine it. The tropics are real, though an Eskimo who's never traveled can't grasp them.

And heaven is real even if we have a hard time envisioning it. But there's good news—God has told us enough that we *can* begin to do just that. In fact, as we'll see in the next chapter, much of what he tells us is surprisingly familiar. We *do* have the necessary earthly reference points to gain a significant—though incomplete—understanding of heaven.

It's difficult to desire something you can't imagine. That's exactly why Satan works so hard to eclipse the biblical teaching on heaven. He keeps us from desiring heaven by keeping us from imagining it—or prompting us to imagine it in all the wrong ways.

Will You Be Amazed?

"It's so *huge,*" Dani tells her angelic guide, Torel, in *Dominion.* But Torel can't get over Dani's astonishment:

> "It is exactly the size Elyon told you it would be. Did you not read Elyon's Book where he laid out the precise measurements of the eternal city?
>
> "I am confounded at all the things your people were plainly told in Elyon's Word but which you act amazed about when you get here. Will you also be amazed to find flowing water, trees, brilliant jewels, and golden streets polished to appear like transparent glass? I can understand why *seeing* such things would amaze you. But to be surprised at their very existence when Elyon revealed them to you is beyond my understanding."

One of my goals in writing *Deadline, Dominion,* and *Edge of Eternity* was the same as the central purpose for this book: motivating people to think more about heaven and to anticipate it with greater fervor and delight.

If you investigate the Scripture passages noted in this book, you may discover to your surprise that many of your assumptions about heaven are not biblical.

How about you—when you get to heaven, how astonished will you be by the tangible existence of what Scripture told us beforehand?

Will you be surprised to see that heaven is an actual place? It's a location that has been traveled to and from by Christ (John 6:33; Acts 1:2), by angels (Matthew 28:2; Revelation 10:1), and in rare circumstances by people prior to their deaths (2 Kings 2:11; 2 Corinthians 12:2; Revelation 11:12).

Where is heaven? It's referred to as "up" in location (Mark 6:41; Luke 9:51). It could be a place in the universe beyond the earth. Or it may exist entirely outside our space-time continuum.

Will you be amazed to see an actual city in heaven? Heaven is described as a city in Hebrews (11:16; 12:22; 13:14) and Revelation (21:1-2). The normal understanding of *city* is a place of many residences in near proximity, with inhabitants under a common government.

This city at the center of the future heaven is called the New Jerusalem. The city's exact dimensions are measured by an angel (Revelation 21:15-17) and reported to be cube-shaped, with each side measuring twelve thousand stadia (nearly fifteen hundred miles).

While these proportions may have symbolic importance, this doesn't mean they aren't literal. In fact, Revelation 21 expresses these exact dimensions with care and emphasizes that they are in "man's measurement" (21:17). If the city really has these dimensions (and there's no reason it couldn't), what more could we expect God to say to convince us?

The base of the city adds up to more than two million square miles. A metropolis of that size in the middle of the United States would stretch from Canada to Mexico and from the Appalachian Mountains to the California border.

Even more astounding is its fifteen-hundred-mile height. That would be about 780,000 stories high. Perhaps this is the reach of the city's tallest towers and spires, rising above buildings of lesser but equally impressive height.

The dimensions of the city often are cited as proof that it isn't a literal city at all. A theology professor told me, "No one can breathe fifteen hundred miles off the ground; there's no oxygen." But why would it be a problem for God to make it so our new bodies don't require oxygen or to extend the atmosphere of the new earth above fifteen hundred miles?

Others say there can't actually be twelve gates of the city made of single pearls (Revelation 21:21). "If the pearls are that big, how big are the oysters?" But again, why would this be a problem for God? An omnipotent Creator can certainly make pearls as big as he wants! Our limited vision of heaven flows out of our limited vision of God.

Will you be amazed to see heaven's earthlike beauty? The New Jerusalem will be filled with visual magnificence, including streets of gold and buildings of pearls, emeralds, and precious stones (Revelation 21:19-21).

Heaven has light, water, trees, and fruit (Revelation 22:1-2). It contains some animals—including wolves, lambs, and lions—

in its millennial phase at least (Isaiah 65:25). Even before the millennium, there are enough horses in heaven (Revelation 6:2-8; 19:11) for the armies of heaven to ride (Revelation 19:14; 2 Kings 6:17).

Other animals aren't mentioned in these passages, presumably because they don't play a role in Christ's second coming. But it seems likely that since there are innumerable horses in heaven, there are all kinds of other animals too.

(I'm often asked whether I think our pets will be in heaven, so I'll interject a brief answer. I once read Billy Graham's response to a little girl's question, "Will my dog who died this week be in heaven?" He replied, "If it would make you any happier, then yes, he will be." Animals aren't nearly as valuable as people and they don't have eternal souls, but God is their maker and has touched many people's lives through them. It would be simple for him to recreate a pet in heaven if this would bring his children joy.)

Apparently it's within the vast and beautiful New Jerusalem we'll find the personal dwelling places Jesus has prepared for us (John 14:2; Luke 16:9; Revelation 21:2). Like the current earthly Jerusalem, the city will be a melting pot of ethnic diversity, with those of "every nation, tribe, people and language" (Revelation 7:9; see 5:9). But unlike today's Jerusalem, all these people will be united by their common worship of King Jesus.

The city's gates are said to be always open, and people will travel in and out, some bringing glorious items into the city (Revelation 21:24-25; 22:14). This outside travel suggests the city is not the whole of heaven, but merely its center. The gates that are opposite each other will be fifteen hundred miles apart, allowing access from every direction (Luke 13:29). Even the inside will be a huge area to investigate. The gates will lead out to an entire planet, the new earth, and a cosmos with vast realms to explore.

Perhaps it will be a center for arts and culture and large gatherings and events…and maybe some great restaurants, since we know that in heaven we'll be eating and drinking (Luke 22:30) and even "feasting" (Matthew 8:11). Heaven's capital city will have all the advantages we associate with earthly cities but none of the disadvantages. No crime, no litter, no smog, no sirens, no seaminess and corruption. The streets can be walked safely.

I've had Christians say to me, "I hate the idea of living in a city." Don't make the mistake of imposing on God's city what you don't like about sin-tarnished earthly cities. His city will allow privacy without isolation, accessibility without suspicion, safety without firearms, provisions without stockpiling, society without bureaucracy. Every stranger could soon be your friend. Heaven will be a vibrant community, a new place populated by new people.

Many assume heaven will be unlike earth. But why do we think this? God designed earth for human beings. And nearly every description of heaven includes references to earthly things—eating, music, animals, water, trees, fruits, and a city with gates and streets.

The Bible speaks of the new heavens and the new earth—not a *non*heavens and *non*earth. "New" doesn't mean fundamentally different, but vastly superior. If someone says, "I'm going to give you a new car," you'd get excited. Why? Not because you have no idea what a car is, but because you *do* know.

31

A new car doesn't mean a vehicle without a steering wheel, seats, doors, and tires. If it didn't have those, it wouldn't be a car. The new car is a better version of what you already have. Likewise, the new earth will be a far better version of this earth. That's why we can anticipate it. If we think of heaven as a place where disembodied spirits float around—which is never depicted in the Bible—we can't get excited about it. It's not a nonearth we long for—it's a *new* earth. And we long not for a nonbody but for a *new* body (2 Corinthians 5:1-4).

It's as Lord Digory explained to the children in C. S. Lewis's *Chronicles of Narnia:* "Our own world…is only a shadow or copy of something in Aslan's real world."

The promise of new heavens and a new earth is introduced in Isaiah (65:17-19; 66:22). In the New Testament, John tells us more about it (Revelation 21), and Peter speaks of the earth being burned, followed by "a new heaven and a new earth, the home of righteousness" (2 Peter 3:10-13). I understand this not as the absolute destruction of the planet, but the scorching of the surface and everything on it. It's as if an artist wiped paint away and started a new and better painting, but on the same canvas. As our resurrection bodies will be a superior recreation of our old ones, so the new earth will be the old earth liberated from sin and decay (Romans 8:19-22), radically and beautifully transformed.

Our beloved, Jesus, and our home, heaven. What a person! What a place! (What more could we possibly ask for?)

Meanwhile we should live our lives on earth in light of eternity, as our spiritual forefathers did, anticipating the great city that awaits us:

By faith Abraham, when called to go to a place he would later receive as his inheritance, obeyed and went, even though he did not know where he was going. By faith he made his home in the promised land like a stranger in a foreign country; he lived in tents, as did Isaac and Jacob, who were heirs with him of the same promise. For he was looking forward to the city with foundations, whose architect and builder is God. (Hebrews 11:8-10)

We are strangers in a foreign country called earth. We live in tents, feeble temporary dwellings, but we're headed toward glorious permanence.

We live on shifting sand, but we look forward every day to the city with foundations—the city that will never fall; the city whose builder and maker is none other than our bridegroom…the Carpenter from Nazareth.

When Aslan's creatures leave Narnia and enter heaven, one of them proclaims words that will be our heart cry when we relocate from earth to heaven:

"I have come home at last! This is the land I have been looking for all my life, though I never knew it till now. The reason why we loved the old Narnia is that it sometimes looked a little like this."

He Knows How to Build

When I anticipate my first glimpse of heaven, I think of the first time I went snorkeling.

Etched in my memory is a certain sound. It's a gasp going through my rubber snorkel as my eyes first took in the breathtaking underwater scene. There were countless fish of every shape, size, and color. And just when I thought I'd seen the most beautiful, along came another even more striking.

After snorkeling in the shallows, I ventured farther out into sixty-foot water, so clear I had the sensation of falling. I could see fish far below as if only a few feet away.

For most of my life I'd never thought about that underwater world. But I fell in love with it that week; I look at underwater pictures hanging on my office wall and often find myself thinking of that world.

I imagine our first glimpse of heaven will cause us to gasp in amazement and delight. That first gasp is likely to be followed by many more as we continually encounter new sights in that endlessly wonderful place.

Ironically, the first verse concerning heaven that comes to

many people's minds is one they imagine discourages thoughts about heaven. "No eye has seen, no ear has heard, no mind has conceived what God has prepared for those who love him" (1 Corinthians 2:9). It sounds wonderful, but it appears to be a conversation stopper. Until, that is, you read the next verse, which actually completes the sentence: "but God has revealed it to us by his Spirit."

The things God has prepared for us that no human mind could have discerned have been revealed to us by his Spirit. Where? In his Word. It doesn't tell us everything, but if we look carefully, it tells us a great deal.

Why will heaven be so beautiful and wonderful? Because the One who's prepared it for us is so skillful and creative.

Knowing our children were coming, Nanci and I prepared a place for them. We chose the room, picked out the right wall-paper, decorated and set up the crib just so, selected the perfect blankets. The quality of the place we prepared for our daughters was limited only by our skills and resources and imaginations.

Since our Lord isn't limited in any of those categories, and since he loves us even more than we love our children, what kind of a place can we expect him to have prepared for us? It will simply be the best place ever made by anyone and for anyone.

In *Edge of Eternity,* Christ is represented by the Woodsman, who sacrifices himself while placing a tree bridge across a bottomless chasm. Shortly thereafter the Woodsman comes alive and carries Nick, the book's main character, across the chasm.

On the other side, Nick continues his journey toward Charis, the City of Light, and tells us of the Woodsman's encouragement:

"But why is it still so far away?" I asked, pointing to the west.

"At moments Charis will seem close to you; sometimes it will seem impossibly far. But every day on the red road you will be one day closer to it. I am building a home for you. I'll be there to welcome you when you arrive."

My heart sang and sank in the same moment.

"You're leaving me, then?"

"I'll be inside." He put his hand on my chest. "And I'll give you instructions to show you the way."

"The place you said you're building for me…what will it be like?"

"A home made just for you. You'll like it." He smiled. "I know how to build."

Our home is being built for us by the Carpenter from Nazareth. Building is his trade. A good carpenter envisions what he wants to build. He plans and designs. Then he does his work, carefully and skillfully fashioning it to exact specifications. He takes pride in the work he's done and delights to show it to others. And when it's his own children or his bride he's made it for, he takes special delight.

Jesus didn't say to his disciples, "I've already prepared a place for you in heaven," but, "I am going there to prepare a place for you." This means heaven has undergone some remodeling between the time he spoke and the time we join him there.

In the Bible, there are at least five distinct phases of heaven. There was the original pre-sin heaven, before Satan fell (Isaiah

14:12-15; Ezekiel 28:12-17), taking perhaps a third of the angels with him (Revelation 12:4,9).

There was the Old Testament heaven of Paradise or "Abraham's bosom" (Luke 16:22, KJV), which was then one of two compartments of Sheol (Hebrew) or Hades (Greek), "the place of the dead." (The other compartment was an earlier form of hell.)

Then came the current postresurrection-of-Christ heaven, where Paradise seems to have been relocated from Hades, and where believers now come directly into the Lord's presence at death (Ephesians 4:8-10; 2 Corinthians 5:8).

The millennial kingdom, where Christ will rule over the earth with his redeemed—but where there will still be some mortal men with sin in their hearts—seems to be a further phase (Revelation 20:7-10). This appears to be the time when "the wolf and the lamb will feed together.... They will neither harm nor destroy on all my holy mountain, says the LORD" (Isaiah 65:25).

Then there is the heaven still to come after the final judgment—the New Jerusalem in the new heavens and new earth (Revelation 21–22). There at last everyone will be in their resurrection bodies, and there will be no more sin or death.

Similarly, what we now refer to as hell (the only compartment of Hades still remaining) will itself be relocated, after the Great White Throne judgment, into the eternal lake of fire, the true and final hell (Revelation 20:14-15).

Heaven is not yet as it one day will be, just as all of creation is not yet as it one day will be. There is still sin and suffering in the universe that will not be relieved until after the present heaven and earth pass away and the new ones are formed (Revelation

21:4-5). God may renovate heaven yet again for all we know. Perhaps there will be continuous building projects. Maybe some of us will be the Carpenter's apprentices, working alongside him.

If we fail to understand these different phases of heaven, it will make no sense to us when we read there are still "spiritual forces of evil in the heavenly realms" (Ephesians 6:12). It will seem contradictory to see Satan coming before the presence of God in Job 1:6 and to be told that in the future "war in heaven" Satan will be cast down (Revelation 12:7). ("But wasn't he already cast down, in Isaiah 14?") These passages show the judgment on Satan did not happen all at once, but it has phases. His final defeat takes place a thousand years after he's bound in the pit when, after one last rage of evil, he will be thrown forever into the lake of fire (Revelation 20:2-3,7-10).

The resurrection of believers won't occur until just prior to the new heavens and earth (Revelation 20:11-15). So even though the present heaven we enter at death is a wonderful place, it's not yet in its most glorious form.

When we die, provided we have accepted Christ's gift of salvation, we go to a place wonderful beyond imagination...but thanks to the Master Carpenter, it's a place that will one day be better still.

Seven

What's Most Important About Heaven?

What's the most important fact about our future home? This is it: Heaven is the place God lives (Deuteronomy 26:15; Matthew 6:9). It's where he sits on the throne and dwells in all his holiness (Revelation 4:2-8; Isaiah 6). Heaven contains an actual sanctuary—God's dwelling place—which served as the pattern for the earthly tabernacle (Hebrews 8:5; 9:11,23-24).

In heaven there's a temple that contains the prototype ark of the covenant (Revelation 11:19, 15:5), another fact that violates the popular notion of a "spiritual" heaven with no physical form.

Heaven is where Christ came from (John 6:42), where he returned to (Acts 1:11), where he now is and from which he will return to earth (Acts 1:11; Revelation 19:11-16).

In the new heavens and earth, "The dwelling of God is with men, and he will live with them. They will be his people, and God himself will be with them and be their God" (Revelation 21:3). This will be an unprecedented joining of heaven and earth, which have always been separate. The new earth is the cosmic center of the new heavens. It will be, literally, heaven on earth.

Notice the text doesn't say God will take men up to make our dwelling in his world. Rather, it says God will come down to make *his* dwelling in *our* world. Going to heaven is not our going to a spiritual realm made by God for himself, a realm in which we won't really fit. Rather, it's God coming to enter a physical realm created by him for us, a realm in which we'll perfectly fit.

We humans are a hybrid of the spiritual and physical (Genesis 2:7). We're made for a world that incorporates both. The bodies he made for us aren't a mistake, but a sovereign design. We don't change our species when we go to heaven—we become all our Creator intended men and women to be. Finally liberated from sin and death, we arrive in the place he's lovingly prepared for us, eager to walk with him and be introduced to the world he's made for us.

Jesus currently "serves in the sanctuary, the true tabernacle set up by the Lord, not by man" (Hebrews 8:2). Heaven is also the place where Christ promised his followers they would live with him (John 12:26; 13:36; 14:2-3). In my novel *Deadline*, the character Finney, having just entered heaven, meets his Savior face to face:

> At the back of the crowd stood one being glowing with a soft light that did not blind, but attracted and captivated the eyes. He smiled at Finney, who trembled with joy at the immediate realization of who it was.
>
> This was the ageless one, the Ancient of Days, who is eternally young. He stepped forward…. He who had spun the galaxies into being with a single snap of his finger, he who could uncreate all that existed with no more than a thought, extended his hand to Finney, as if the hand he

extended was that of a plain ordinary carpenter.... For the moment, it was impossible to look elsewhere, and no one in his right mind would have wanted to.

"Welcome, my son! Enter the kingdom prepared for you, by virtue of a work done by another, a work you could not do. Here you shall receive reward for those works you did in my name, works you were created to do."

And then, with a smile that communicated more than any smile Finney had ever seen, the Great One looked into his eyes and said with obvious pride, "Well done my good and faithful servant. Enter into the joy of your Lord!"

As the crowd broke out in cheers, Finney felt over-whelmed and dropped to his knees, then flat on the ground, face down, as if the knees were still too lofty a position before the Lord of Heaven.

The Bible tells us heaven is the dwelling place not only of God but also of his angels (Luke 2:15; Matthew 28:2; Hebrews 12:22). Furthermore, it's the residence of God's saints from earth who have died and now live in his presence (Revelation 4:4, 10-11; 5:6,8; Luke 16:22,25; Hebrews 12:23).

Heaven will always be *our* home, because it is *God's* home, and we are God's family.

The most amazing aspect of heaven is expressed in Revelation 22:4, which says of God's servants, "They will see his face."

There's no way to describe what a shocking statement this is to any Jew trained in the transcendence and unapproachability of God. The Creator said to Moses, "you cannot see my face, for no one may see me and live" (Exodus 33:20). The high priest could go into the Holy of Holies only once a year, and even then tradition says a rope was tied around his ankle in case God struck him down. (Who would dare go in to get him?)

The God who lives in unapproachable light became approachable in the person of Jesus (John 1:14). Though we will always be creature and he Creator, in heaven we will be able to live with him and actually "see his face." Incredible.

David anticipated seeing God's face in heaven (Psalm 17:15). His prayer was "that I may dwell in the house of the LORD all the days of my life, to gaze upon the beauty of the LORD" (Psalm 27:4). We will experience the answer to David's prayer. God's house will be our home.

From this Most Important Fact springs a cluster of other vital facts about heaven:

Because God's home is our home, heaven contains his permanent inheritance for us, an unperishing estate he has reserved for us (1 Peter 1:4).

Because God's home is our home, the names of Christ's redeemed are written in heaven (Luke 10:20; Hebrews 12:23; Revelation 20:15).

Because God's home is our home, the wicked, those whose sins remain uncleansed by the blood of Christ, will be excluded from heaven (Galatians 5:21; Ephesians 5:5; Revelation 22:15). Those who refuse to acknowledge the Master of the house are not welcome in it.

Because God's home is our home, heaven is our country of citizenship (Hebrews 11:16; Philippians 3:20). During our brief stay here on earth, we are pilgrims (Hebrews 11:13).

The black slaves in early America had something we should learn from—a pilgrim mentality. With minimal possessions and power, they lived for another world, a better one. This central theme permeated their spirituals. They sang, "I am a poor way-farin' stranger, a-travelin' far away from home." "Soon I will be done with the troubles of the world; I'm goin' home to live with God." "Swing low, sweet chariot, comin' for to carry me home."

The more possessions and power we have in this world, the more tempted we are to forget our true citizenship is in heaven.

Because God's home is our home, Christ is our King, and we're now his ambassadors, representing his agenda on earth (2 Corinthians 5:20).

Imagine an ambassador who leaves his country to live in another nation hostile to his own. Naturally he'll want to learn the language, see the sights, eat the food, become familiar with the people and culture. But suppose he fails to draw the line. Suppose he becomes so engrossed in this country's customs and philosophies that he gradually assimilates into it. He becomes sympathetic to its policies, buys into its values, begins to regard it as his home.

His allegiance wavers. He compromises his position as an ambassador. He becomes increasingly ineffective in representing the best interests of his true country. At best, he becomes incapable of serving his true country. At worst, he may actually betray it. He may defect.

His fatal mistake was this: Just because he lived somewhere, he came to think of it as his home. As Christians, we live on earth, but earth is not our home.

How are you doing as an ambassador for Christ? How are you doing representing your true country, heaven, as you live in this world that's not yours? Have you adopted values and customs of this culture that are contrary to those of the culture of heaven? Have you compromised your allegiance to your true country and your true King?

God describes his ambassadors this way:

> All these people were still living by faith when they died. They did not receive the things promised; they only saw them and welcomed them from a distance. And they admitted that they were aliens and strangers on earth. People who say such things show that they are looking for a country of their own. If they had been thinking of the country they had left, they would have had opportunity to return. Instead, they were longing for a better country—a heavenly one. Therefore God is not ashamed to be called their God, for he has prepared a city for them. (Hebrews 11:13-16)

Are you ashamed to call God your God? Is God ashamed to be called your God? Are you thinking of the city God has prepared for you? Are you "longing for a better country"? Are you living now in light of all that country means?

Perhaps we should say aloud, over and over, the words of the black spirituals: "This world is not my home, this world is not my home, this world is not my home…."

Eight

What Will We Be Like in Heaven?

One of Satan's great myths about heaven is that we'll be so different there, we won't really be us.

Torel reminds Dani in *Dominion,* "It is *you* in heaven, not some new creature that did not exist on earth. The same person who steps out of earth is the one who steps into heaven."

People in heaven are called by name—Abraham and Isaac and Jacob (Matthew 8:11) and Lazarus (Luke 16:25). A name denotes a distinct identity, an individual personality. The fact that it's the same name used on earth demonstrates we'll be the same people. I'll be Randy Alcorn throughout eternity, just without the bad parts. You'll be who you are throughout eternity, just without the bad parts.

That we'll also be given a new name (Revelation 2:17) shows our unique personalities will grow, as new names reflect the parent's aspirations for the child or his observation of notable traits. That only we will know this new name shows there's privacy in heaven—some things will be held uniquely between God and us. That we'll have private thoughts demonstrates heaven won't involve the loss of individual identity. We won't dissolve into some Nirvana-like cosmic consciousness.

As our genetic code and fingerprints are unique now, we should expect they will be in our new bodies. Individual identity is an essential aspect of personhood. Resurrection isn't reincarnation as someone else; it's a rebuilding of ourselves.

Dani held a common misconception. "I had thought," she told Torel, "that in heaven we'd be spirits without bodies."

> Torel looked at her as if this were ludicrous. "How could that be? Have you not read that Elyon created a body, then breathed into it a spirit, and only when there was both body and spirit was there a living human being? To be human is to be both spirit and body. To cease to be either is to cease to be human.… You do not become inhuman in heaven. Rather, you become *fully* human—all that Elyon intended that you should be."

There were human beings before sin, and there will be fully human beings after sin—far *better* human beings, but never *non*-human beings. We'll have everything that makes a person a person.

Children have guardian angels (Matthew 18:10), but contrary to popular myths, they do not *become* angels when they die. People and angels are two different kinds of beings. When humans die, they remain humans.

What will we look like in heaven? We'll look like ourselves. Why? Because we'll *be* ourselves.

Christ's resurrection body is the model and prototype for our own heavenly bodies (1 Corinthians 15:20,48-49; Philippians 3:21; 1 John 3:2). Whatever was true of his resurrection body will presumably be true of ours.

After his resurrection, Jesus emphasized that he was not a "ghost"—a disembodied spirit—but had a physical body (Luke 24:37-39). A few times Jesus wasn't immediately recognized (John 20:15; Luke 24:15-16), suggesting there was some change in his appearance. (Most of us would welcome *some* change in our appearance, wouldn't we?) Then, after being with him awhile, his disciples suddenly recognized him (John 20:16; Luke 24:31). This suggests that despite any change in outer appearance, the inner identity of people may shine through.

This perceptible inner reality is what I portrayed in *Deadline:*

Finney looked at his welcoming party and wondered if they were wearing special attire or if this was simply the standard dress of heaven. Yet actually he wasn't sure this was clothing at all. It seemed at first like white robes, dazzlingly bright yet not hurtful to his eyes. But each person's appearance was distinctly different from the other. The similarity spoke of their shared purity and common Lord and the differences of their unique personalities and gifts and histories.

But the clothing, if that's what it was, seemed more an organic growth from the body than separate apparel. Rather than concealing, it seemed designed to reveal something which on earth would have been hidden within. When he looked at an individual he seemed to see so much more than he'd ever seen before. On earth the outward appearance could deceive and often did. But here the outward appearance seemed to reflect and draw attention to the inner person, to his or her character. And somehow Finney caught hints and impressions of the person's unique background and history.

This may help with the common questions, "Will those who die as children be children in heaven? Will the elderly still appear old?" God could make everyone appear to be thirty years old, but I don't expect that kind of uniformity. I imagine those who die old will be young again—certainly they will not be weak or frail. Because of God's special love for children, I envision children all over heaven, running in meadows and playing with animals and laughing and singing and worshiping their King. (We know from Isaiah 11:8-9 that during the millennial phase of heaven there will be children playing near animals that won't harm them.)

In my novels I suggest parents may see their children as young, and children see their parents as older. Perhaps at times we'll be adults, according to the place and purposes and companions we're with, then be transformed to children and back again. I expect heaven won't be a place of "no ages" but of "all ages."

In our resurrected state we'll have real "spiritual" bodies with physical substance (1 Corinthians 15:42-44). We'll be capable of talking, walking, touching, and being touched. Christ's resurrection body had an ability to appear suddenly, apparently coming through a locked door to the apostles (John 20:19), and disappear from sight just as quickly, as during his sojourn with the two disciples near Emmaus (Luke 24:31). Christ ascended into heaven in his new body (Acts 1:9). This suggests we may be able to fly and otherwise transcend the present laws of physics.

Christ ate food in his resurrection body, and both he and we will eat and drink in heaven (Luke 14:15; 22:18). Most of us like to eat and drink. Every reference to sitting at a table and having a banquet in heaven should forever free us from the myth of floating around like ghosts (Isaiah 25:6).

Though we'll eat and drink, there will be no hunger or thirst in heaven (Revelation 7:16). Our heavenly bodies apparently won't need what is now essential—food, drink, oxygen, covering—but we'll be fully capable of enjoying these things.

Between the time of our entrance to heaven and our resurrection, I think there are strong indications we may be given temporary preresurrection bodies. Immediately after death the rich man and Lazarus are described in physical terms, with references to "his finger" and "my tongue" and "cool water" (Luke 16:19-26). Those who have just died and entered heaven—prior to the resurrection—are said to be wearing robes, indicating they have physical bodies (Revelation 6:11). We are told that at death, not just at the resurrection, we will leave our earthly bodies "to be clothed with our heavenly dwelling" (2 Corinthians 5:1-4).

Unlike God and the angels—who are in essence spirits, though capable of inhabiting bodies (John 4:24; Hebrews 1:14)—human beings are in essence both spiritual and physical (Genesis 2:7). A temporary body would allow us to retain the qualities of full humanity between death and resurrection, when we will be joined to our ultimate bodies.

A godly Christian man once told me that the thought of eating and drinking and physical activities in heaven seemed terribly "unspiritual" to him. But this teaching shouldn't surprise us, since our Creator made us both body and spirit.

Some think we won't be male or female in heaven, based on what Jesus says in Matthew 22:30. ("At the resurrection people will neither marry nor be given in marriage; they will be like the angels in heaven.") But that passage doesn't teach we'll be genderless. Gender is a God-created aspect of humanity. Jesus simply states there'll be no marriage in heaven but the marriage of Christ and his bride. (This doesn't mean we won't have a close and special relationship with our partner from earth.)

Finney takes this up with his angel host, Zyor, in *Deadline:*

> "But I am still a man here, and everyone I see is clearly male or female, more distinctly in fact than on earth. I had thought perhaps there would be no gender here. I had read that we would all be…like angels, like you."
>
> Zyor looked immensely surprised at this.
>
> "You are like us in that you do not marry and bear children here. But as for your being a man, what else would you be? Elyon may unmake what men make, but he does not unmake what *he* makes. He made you male, as he made your mother and wife and daughters female. Gender is not merely a component of your being to be added in or extracted and discarded. It is an essential part of who you are."

Before Mary recognized Jesus in his new body, she addressed him as "Sir," showing she saw him as being male (John 20:15). Why would anyone expect otherwise?

Much of our misunderstanding stems from the Platonic belief that the body is evil and the spirit's highest destiny is to be forever free from the body. But the Bible teaches something Plato didn't grasp—that God is the Creator of both body and spirit, both of which were marred by sin, but both of which are redeemed by Christ.

True, I need to be delivered from my earthly body, which is subject to sin and decay (Romans 7:24). But the promise of heaven isn't the absence of body. Rather, it's the attainment of a new and sinless body and spirit.

In 1 Corinthians 15, Paul regards the new *body*—not simply the new spirit—as essential to our redemption. If the body isn't redeemed, man is not redeemed, since man is by nature body as well as spirit. A spirit without a body, like a body without a spirit, is not the highest human destiny. Rather, it would be a state of incompleteness, an aberration from the full meaning of humanness. Paul speaks of a "spiritual body," which sounds to us like a contradiction in terms because of our erroneous assumptions.

Flowing out of their Platonic assumptions, Christians sometimes talk of the marriage supper (Revelation 19:9) as if it wasn't what a marriage supper really is—a gathering in a place where people eat and drink and dance and talk and laugh. If these things are typical of celebratory suppers here on earth, why wouldn't they be in heaven? Jesus said he would drink wine with his disciples again in heaven (Matthew 26:29). Another figure of speech?

There are figures of speech that convey the joyful excitement of heaven: "You will go out in joy and be led forth in peace; the mountains and hills will burst into song before you, and all the trees of the field will clap their hands" (Isaiah 55:12). That doesn't mean there won't be mountains and trees, but that creation will at last be delivered from the curse (Romans 8:21), a reason for great celebration.

Are all the biblical references to eating and drinking and horses and trees and fruits and streams in heaven symbolic? Symbolic of what? If we were non-physical beings in heaven, maybe there would be some ethereal spiritual truth symbolized by references to feasts and tables and singing and celebrating. But the fact is that we will be physical beings. We are and will be *us*—therefore we need not and should not search for abstract spiritual meanings for things that people like us naturally do.

(Of course Scripture does contain poetic and apocalyptic language, but when the plain meaning could be true, why not just let heaven be what God says rather than gutting it by robbing his words of their meanings?)

"I find," Dani says to Torel in *Dominion,* "that what I experience in heaven is largely an outgrowth of earth. The two aren't disconnected. It's not a new and separate reality as much as an extension of the old reality. My mind is the same mind, only sharper; my soul the same soul, only completely pure. My skills are the same skills, but less hindered in their expression."

Yes, God will change us in heaven—aren't you glad? But he will never obliterate or replace us—aren't you glad for that, too? We'll still be us...but a better us than we can possibly imagine.

Explosion of Joy

Remember the pastor's confession? He thought heaven sounded "so terribly boring" and "not much better than hell."

If that picture's wrong, what exactly will we do in heaven that will make it so enjoyable?

In *Edge of Eternity,* Nick is marooned at the edge of a vast chasm. He hears screams—and nothing more—from the fathomless depths. The screams are from Erebus, the story's name for hell. (Since God's grace is what allows us into heaven, I named heaven "Charis," the Greek word for grace.)

Nick talks with an angelic warrior named Marcus in a discussion that contrasts heaven and hell:

"I hear no conversation in the chasm," I said, my voice shaking.

"There is no one near enough to talk to, nothing to talk about," Marcus said. "Erebus is an endless monologue. What else do you not hear?"

"Music."

"There is none and never will be."

"Not even songs of lamentation?"

"Those who have no hope cannot sing. Charis has a

song for every star. It is a country of explosion, expanding with every song, becoming ever larger."

Marcus stretched out his hand, and the air's fabric ripped open, so I could see above and beyond the abyss and peer into the City of Light as if it were but a few feet away. People laughed, greeted each other, embraced, conversed with animated expressions. I kept hearing the word "Yes!" It struck me as strange, as I'd always believed if there was a heaven it was a place of naysayers.

In Charis I saw citizens busily working, learning, and exploring, overflowing with the joy of discovery. They seemed immersed in delight.

Yes, I knew it was Charis I longed for. Who but a fool would not long for it?

This joy and fulfillment in heaven—in the "country of explosion"—will erupt not only from positive experiences, but also from what is *not* there. No arthritis, no handicaps, no cancer, no mosquitoes, no taxes, no bills, no computer crashes, no weeds, no bombs, no drunkenness, no traffic jams and accidents, no septic tank backups, no door locks, no phone calls selling storm windows at dinnertime. No mental illness. No pretense, no wearing masks. Close friendships but no cliques, laughter but no put-downs. Intimacy, but no temptation to immorality.

What will *not* be there is material decay and corruption (Matthew 6:20).

What will *not* be there is burdensome toil (Revelation 14:13).

What will *not* be there is any more "death or mourning or crying or pain" (Revelation 21:4).

What will *not* be there is the sinful human condition (Romans 7:24), in which all boredom is actually rooted.

Some imagine that in heaven we'll be all dressed up with nowhere to go and nothing to do. (Except take an eternal afternoon nap, strum that harp, and polish that gold.) I've concluded there are two unspoken assumptions behind this pervasive notion that heaven will be boring. The first is that God is boring. (When an omnipotent being creates the ultimate place, if he is exciting, it will be exciting. If the place is dull, it's because he's dull.) The second assumption is that life without sin would not be interesting. The idea is, "What will we do for entertainment if there's no sin?"

The fact that such notions would even occur to us demonstrates the extent to which we're blinded by the evil one. His most basic strategy, exactly the one he employed with Adam and Eve, is to make us think wrongly about God and believe sin will bring us fulfillment.

But sin is not what brings us fulfillment—it's what robs us of fulfillment. Sin isn't what makes life interesting; it's what makes life empty. This emptiness inevitably leads to boredom. When there's fulfillment, when there's beauty, when we see God as he truly is, boredom becomes an impossibility. In heaven we will be *filled*, as Psalm 16:11 describes, "with joy" and "with eternal pleasures." Why? Because God is infinitely rich and pleasure-giving.

Remember our Most Important Fact about heaven? Heaven

is God's home, the dwelling place of the One who is infinite in creativity, goodness, beauty, and power. How could the home of someone like that be anything less than thrilling?

We'll experience what Dani did:

> The wild rush of Joy, the rapture of discovery over-whelmed her as if she'd just gotten in on the greatest inside joke in the history of the universe. Now she saw and felt it with stunning clarity. Her unswerving patriotism had been reserved for another country. Every joy on earth, such as the joy of reunion, had been but an inkling, a whisper of greater Joy. Every place on earth had been a rented room, a place to spend the night on a journey.

Heaven is a place where there's great rejoicing (an emotional response) over what God is accomplishing on earth (Luke 15:7,10). This means we won't lose our capacity for emotions. Revelation 6:10 shows that in heaven we'll be capable of expressing emotions, including righteous anger concerning sin.

Emotions are part of our God-created humanity, not some sinful baggage we're to be cleansed of. We shouldn't expect the absence of emotion in heaven. Rather, we should anticipate pure and accurately informed emotions guided by reality, not subjective feelings that are easily misled.

There's no reason to believe we won't shed tears of joy in heaven—upon meeting Christ, for example, or being reunited with loved ones. The tears to be wiped away (Revelation 21:4) are the tears of suffering over sin and death.

As our joy abounds, we'll no doubt increase both our capacity and our desire for even more.

> "On the one hand I feel so fulfilled, so satisfied," Dani said. "This is Joy—every experience of joy on earth was the stab, the pang, the inconsolable longing for this place. Yet, in a strange way, I feel my desires, my yearnings, my thirst is greater than ever. How can this be?"
>
> "You are experiencing what you were made for," Torel said. "There is thirst because there is water; hunger because there is food. There is spiritual thirst because there is the water that is Elyon, the one for whom you were made. It is a thirst fully satisfied in him, yet which reoccurs in order to draw you back to drink ever more deeply from him."

The joyful redeemed in heaven are described as "shining" and wearing "white robes," indicating their moral purity and righteousness (Daniel 12:3; Matthew 13:43; Revelation 3:4; 6:11). Far from being a deterrent to joy, purity is a source of it.

Our explosion of joy will coincide with the flowering of our righteousness. In that day, we will be amazed that people once imagined temptation and sin were the allies of excitement and fulfillment, when in fact they were their greatest enemies.

What does God say to his faithful servants when their work on earth is done? "Come and share your master's happiness" (Matthew 25:23). The contagious joy of our Lord will permeate every square foot of heaven and every square inch of us.

Ten

Refreshing Rest, Fascinating Labor

Throughout the book of Revelation we see communication, dialogue, corporate worship, and other relationship-building interchange among saints and angels and God. We'll all interact together in heaven, building and deepening relationships.

We'll eat and drink at a table with Christ and the redeemed saints from earth, having fellowship and rejoicing with them (Matthew 8:11; Luke 22:29-30; Revelation 19:9). We'll experience what Nick describes from afar in *Edge of Eternity* when he first glimpses the City of Light: "I saw what seemed to be the radiant energy of people celebrating.... I heard a geyser of laughter exploding from a fountain of joy."

All heaven will be our special home. But Christ says, "In my Father's house are many rooms.... I am going there to prepare a place for you" (John 14:2). Place is singular, but rooms are plural. This suggests Jesus has in mind an individual dwelling for each of us, which is a smaller part of the larger place and is home to us in the most unique sense. ("Room" is a cozy and intimate term.)

I live in Oregon, but when I've been overseas and land in New York, I feel I've come "home," meaning I'm in my home country. Then when I land in Oregon, I'm "home" in a more specific sense. My neighborhood is even more like home. Finally, when I arrive at my house, at the place uniquely mine, I'm really home. But even there I have a special place or two—our bedroom and my office. The Bible's use of various terms such as "new earth," "country," "city," "place," and "rooms" implies such shades of meaning to "home."

The statement I'm about to make surprises people. Ready? It appears to me Scripture teaches that in heaven we'll welcome others into our dwelling places—we'll open our homes to guests.

After speaking of the shrewd servant's desire to use earthly resources so that "people will welcome me into their houses," Jesus told his followers to use "worldly wealth" (earthly resources) to "gain friends" (by making a difference in their lives on earth). The reason? "So that when it is gone [when life on earth is over], you will be welcomed into eternal dwellings" (Luke 16:9).

Our "friends" in heaven appear to be those whose lives we've touched on earth and who now have their own "eternal dwellings." Luke 16:9 seems to say these "eternal dwellings" of our friends are places where we stay and fellowship, perhaps as we move about the heavenly kingdom.

Because of erroneous assumptions about heaven—mainly that it can't be earthlike—most people don't take Luke 16 literally. They think "eternal dwellings" is a general reference to heaven. But surely Christ isn't saying we'll enter heaven because of how wisely we use our money. In the parable, the eternal dwellings are heaven's equivalent to the individual earthly dwellings, private homes that the man could stay in. Unless there's some compelling reason to interpret this figuratively—and I see none at all—shouldn't we take it at face value?

I can't meditate on this passage without thinking of the joy we'll have in meeting those whose lives we've had a part in, including many we never met on earth. Ray Boltz's song "Thank You" pictures us meeting people in heaven who explain how our ministry and giving touched their lives. They say, "Thank you for giving to the Lord, I am so glad you gave." This is more than just a nice sentiment. It's something that will actually happen. Every time we give to world missions and famine relief I consider this—which is just one of the reasons you couldn't pay me enough not to give.

That we'll visit and share fellowship with those we've impacted on earth indicates we'll recognize and know each other in heaven. Shouldn't that be obvious? Our mental capacities will be sharpened, not dulled (1 Corinthians 13:12). We won't be dumber in heaven; we'll be smarter.

Scripture gives no indication of a "memory wipe" causing us not to recognize family and friends. In fact, if we wouldn't know our loved ones, the "comfort" of an afterlife reunion taught in 1 Thessalonians 4:14-18 would be pointless.

Matthew 17:1-4 gives further evidence for our recognition of each other in heaven. At Christ's transfiguration, the disciples recognized Moses and Elijah, even though they couldn't have known what they looked like. (No photographs.) This may again suggest personality will emanate through a person's body, so we can instantly recognize people we know *of* but haven't previously met.

Love transcends death (1 Corinthians 13:13). We'll no doubt lose interest in many things that attracted us on earth. It's hard to imagine, for instance, talking about a favorite television program—not because it would be evil, but because it would be so trivial, irrelevant, and dull.

But surely we won't lose interest in the things on earth that mattered, some of which were lighthearted and others deep and profound. These are part of the shared experience of loving relationships. Such adventures forge a camaraderie like that of soldiers who've served beside each other in the trenches. They never forget what they experienced together in that foreign land. Neither, I think, will we forget fighting spiritual battles in the trenches of earth.

I envision us sitting around a campfire telling stories of the truly exciting times on earth, the ones where we turned to our Commander and trusted him to guide and sustain us on the long marches. The ones where we leaned on our comrades for strength, where we tended to each other and carried and guided each other across the minefields. Times when we basked in the company of family and friends, "fellow citizens with God's people and members of God's household" (Ephesians 2:19). (By the way, if you can't imagine sitting around a campfire telling stories in heaven, *why not?*)

We'll worship God alongside the angels and redeemed people from every race and background (Revelation 4:9-11; 7:9-12). We'll play musical instruments in heaven (Revelation 5:8-10; 1 Corinthians 15:52). We'll sing praise songs along with all the rest of God's creation (Revelation 5:13). Since dancing can be a form of worship and celebration on earth (Psalm 149:3), I assume it will be in heaven.

When you're singing in church, expand your mind to anticipate worshiping with the *entire* assembled body of Christ.

Imagine it now, with the following scene from *Edge of Eternity* spurring on your thoughts. The scene occurs on the day Nick observes—and joins—heaven's army in its final cosmic campaign against the forces of darkness.

> We rejoined our comrades in the great camp of Charis, embracing and shedding tears and slapping each other on the back. Then warriors around me turned toward the masses of untold millions gathered in Charis. The army began to sing, perhaps hundreds of thousands, perhaps a million.
>
> I added my voice to theirs and sang the unchained praises of the King. Only for a moment did I hear my own voice, amazed to detect the increased intensity of the whole. One voice, even mine, made a measurable difference. But from then on I was lost in the choir, hardly hearing my voice and not needing to.
>
> As we sang to the gathered throngs of Charis, the sheer power of their voices, our voices, nearly bowled me over.
>
> Then suddenly the multitudes before us sang back to us, and our voices were drowned by theirs. We who a moment earlier seemed the largest choir ever assembled

now proved to be only the small worship ensemble that led the full choir of untold millions, now lost to themselves. We sang together in full voice, "To him who made the galaxies, who became the Lamb, who stretched out on the tree, who crossed the chasm, who returned the Lion! Forever!"

The song's harmonies reached out and grabbed my body and my soul. I became the music's willing captive.

The galaxies and nebulae sang with us the royal song. It echoed off a trillion planets and reverberated in a quadrillion places in every nook and cranny of the universe. The song generated the light of a billion burning supernovae. It blotted out all lesser lights and brought a startling clarity to the way things really were. It didn't blind, it illuminated, and I saw as never before.

Our voices broke into thirty-two distinct parts, and instinctively I knew which of them I was made to sing. "We sing for joy at the work of your hands…we stand in awe of you." It felt indescribably wonderful to be lost in something so much greater than myself.

There was no audience, I thought for a moment, for audience and orchestra and choir all blended into one great symphony, one grand cantata of rhapsodic melodies and powerful sustaining harmonies.

No, wait, there was an audience. An audience so vast and all-encompassing that for a moment I'd been no more aware of it than a fish is aware of water.

I looked at the great throne, and upon it sat the King…the Audience of One.

The smile of his approval swept through the choir like fire across dry wheat fields.

When we completed our song, the one on the throne stood and raised his great arms and clapped his scarred hands together in thunderous applause, shaking ground and sky, jarring every corner of the cosmos. His applause went on and on, unstopping and unstoppable.

And in that moment I knew, with unwavering clarity, that the King's approval was all that mattered—and ever would.

God tells us how we should respond to the coming heaven: "But be glad and rejoice forever in what I will create, for I will create Jerusalem to be a delight and its people a joy. I will rejoice over Jerusalem and take delight in my people" (Isaiah 65:18-19). Reread those two sentences. How much more joy and delight could God have packed into them? We are to rejoice in heaven because he does!

The world is always longing to celebrate, striving to celebrate—it just lacks the true *reasons* to celebrate. We have those reasons…the person and the place. So let's celebrate—let's get a head start on heaven! Don't wait until heaven to start rejoicing (Philippians 4:4).

When at last we arrive in that special place and are with that special person, we'll rest from the labors we knew on earth (Revelation 14:13).

Rest brings its own enjoyment—what feels better than putting your head on the pillow after a hard day's work? (How about after a hard *life's* work?) But the point of rest isn't to vegetate. Rest on earth makes us refreshed and invigorated and ready for what's ahead—we should expect rest in heaven to do exactly the same. That's good news for most of us who *like* to be active and do a lot, provided we have the energy.

Our labor in heaven will be refreshing, productive, and unthwarted—like Adam and Eve's work in Eden before sin brought the curse on the ground (Genesis 3:17-19).

We'll lead and exercise authority in heaven, making important decisions. We'll reign with Christ (2 Timothy 2:12; Revelation 3:21), not temporarily but "for ever and ever" (Revelation 22:5). *Reigning* implies specific delegated responsibilities for those under our leadership (Luke 19:17-19). We'll rule over the world and even over angels (1 Corinthians 6:2-3).

In heaven, we're told we'll serve God (Revelation 7:15). "His servants will serve him" (Revelation 22:3). This is definitive biblical proof we'll be active in heaven. Why? Because "serve" has a meaning—it means to work, to expend effort, to do something. Service involves responsibilities, duties, effort, planning, and creativity to do work well.

These verses should forever refute the poisonous propaganda of eternal passivity that Satan uses to diminish our thirst for heaven.

As Torel tells Dani in *Dominion*, because good is "multifaceted and deep, heaven is therefore endlessly fascinating."

Eleven

Made for Another World

The heaven portrayed in *Edge of Eternity* is "unfathomable... unbridled...boundless adventure."

When I ponder the adventure that awaits us there, the joys and the fellowship, my thoughts drift to my friend Jerry Hardin.

In 1965, as sixth graders, we became best friends. We spent our "wonder years" together. Side by side we patrolled our turf, a few rural Oregon miles of rolling hills, open fields, and sporadic houses. Today, more than thirty years later, I ride my bike over the same ground. Every corner, every driveway, every house and field triggers memories of a time in my life inseparable from Jerry.

Out in those fields, hidden from the rest of the world, he and I engaged enemy soldiers, hunted wild animals, dug up treasures, and encountered aliens. Sometimes I still walk around our little grade school where we spent so much time shooting baskets, throwing footballs, playing catch, and riding our bikes. Then on Friday nights we got civilized, spiffed up, and went to junior high parties together, reeking of Jade East and Brut, intended to make us irresistible to the girls. (They never fell under the spell.)

Every summer we'd go together to the county fair, proving

our emerging manhood by proudly enduring all the scariest rides. We'd eat corn dogs and cotton candy till we were sick. We threw dimes and won goldfish and carnival glass and stuffed animals, first for our moms, then for our girlfriends. One summer, imagining we were cool (trust me, it required a lot of imagination), we wore those stupid Nehru shirts with the high collars, the ones that were in fashion maybe two weeks.

Most Saturdays we went to the Hood Theater, watching matinees now relegated to the oldies section in video stores. Some of the titles still make me think of the guy who shared those giant tubs of popcorn with me as we watched and snickered and exchanged inane comments. I've taken my own teenagers to that same theater, virtually unchanged. The same jujubes and Good & Plenty Jerry and I dropped are still stuck to the floor right where we left them. Certain seats in the balcony still trigger the time warp that takes me back to those years so closely linked to Jerry.

Favorite places. Unforgettable adventures. On display in my mind is an endless collage of games, journeys, field trips, concerts, awards assemblies, and countless little vignettes containing Jerry. Like the eighth-grade musical where Jerry had the lead and I shared the final scene with him. At the climactic moment he ran to the big heavy hanging microphone where he was to burst into song. But he'd miscalculated and couldn't stop in time. He smashed his head on the mike, causing it to swing back and forth like one of Tarzan's tree vines. All the horrified parents and family in the audience didn't deter me from laughing uncontrollably for twenty minutes. Memorable mishaps like that, accumulated over the years of childhood and adolescence, are the bricks and mortar of a unique sort of friendship, the kind those who first meet as adults can't know. Best friends aren't always your oldest ones, but there can never be any friends like early ones.

I remember Jerry and me picking (and throwing) berries at dawn on summer mornings, then spending our afternoons swimming and listening to the Beach Boys and Simon & Garfunkel, switching channels on our squawky eight-transistor radios and reading comic books starring Superman and Batman, who epitomized male strength and heroism. We'd talk about cute girls and adventures and exploits and what we'd do when we grew up. We'd haul out our sleeping bags and camp out under the stars in my backyard with Champ, my golden retriever. We'd look through my telescope at Jupiter's moons and Saturn's rings and the great galaxy of Andromeda and wonder what life was all about. (In those days we didn't know.)

Our eighth-grade year, Jerry made wide receiver and I made quarterback. On weekends, we'd walk from his house to mine, throwing the football back and forth, dreaming dreams of victory. (Few of these ever materialized, but shared dreams create their own bond.) After working up a sweat, we'd make the trek to Miller's Store and share a bottle of Byerly's orange soda.

We excitedly watched them build a brand-new high school right between our houses. We'd be the first four-year graduating class, experiencing and defining the school from its inception. In that freshman year, Jerry and I met the girls we'd later marry, his Carol and my Nanci.

Something else happened in high school, something that would forever shape and transform our friendship. Jerry and I became Christians. Now we spoke of new dreams, loftier ones, informed by new realities. Our deep friendship became permanent not just in sentiment, but in fact. Now we were brothers in an eternal sense.

Soon after getting married, Jerry and I and our wives drove together in a Volkswagen bug on a two-week vacation in California. In the following years we played tennis, talked theology, shared our hopes and struggles. As we raised our children and got deeply involved in our churches and work, the demands of life dictated we spend less time together, but every time we met, often on the tennis court, we picked up exactly where we left off. He was always the same man—steady, consistent, quietly faithful. As dependable as Big Ben and Oregon rain.

I served on the planning committee for our twenty-year high school reunion. I asked if Jerry could speak to our class the first night of the reunion. There was a special reason. At age thirty-eight, Jerry was dying of cancer.

Chemotherapy had left him bald. As I blearily watched him speak that night, I prayed that his words of faith and hope would make a deep impact on our old classmates. They did.

After Jerry was diagnosed as terminal, he and I talked about suffering, healing, and heaven. I picked out lots of books for him, and he read them all. We talked about God's grace in giving him time to prepare for what awaits every one of us. We prayed together for his wife and children. He'd lived well and didn't have to make many changes to be ready to die and meet his Creator. I told him that.

Only a month before he died we played tennis together the

last time. When I lost a point, he'd accuse me of going easy on him. When I won, he'd accuse me of taking advantage of a man dying of cancer. We laughed and kidded each other as only the best of friends can.

God forged our lives together in the same foundry, beginning years before I knew there was a God. That kind of history links two souls. In a strange combination of pain and pleasure, in our last times together we sensed the earthly phase of our friendship drawing to completion. In our final coherent conversation, after I'd read to him a number of Bible passages, I said to Jerry, "We were made for another world, not this one." He smiled and said with a weak voice, full of conviction, "Amen."

Jerry got steadily worse. His family brought him home from the hospital, as he desired. On a Thursday morning I headed to the airport for a speaking engagement in Philadelphia. I decided to leave home an hour early and drop by to see Jerry.

While Nanci sat with Carol in another room, I went to Jerry alone. I hunkered up close to him and read him the last two chapters of the Bible, the same passage I'd read to my mother many times when she was dying. (It was eleven years to the day since she died.) As I read Revelation 21:4, "[God] will wipe every tear from their eyes," I looked up and saw tears in Jerry's eyes. I wiped them away.

I continued to read, through my own tears, right up till Revelation 22:17. "The Spirit and the bride say, 'Come!' And let him who hears say, 'Come!' Whoever is thirsty, let him come; and whoever wishes, let him take the free gift of the water of life."

Between the time I started reading that verse and the time I finished, something powerful and wonderful happened. Jerry went home.

My friend left his temporary residence, his interim home away from Home. One moment he was laboriously breathing the stale air of earth, the next he was effortlessly inhaling the fresh air of heaven.

I had the privilege of being there the moment he walked through that door between two worlds. I had the privilege of saying the last words he heard in this world. The fact that they were God's words, and a specific invitation to come to heaven, heightened my sense of honor in being with Jerry in life's most defining moment, the moment of death. I was there when he signed his life's portrait, when the paint dried, the picture was hung, and the artist went on to bigger and better things. I could almost hear a voice in the world next door, someone saying to my friend, "Well done." (Those who've read *Deadline* will notice I patterned Finney's death after Jerry's.)

I'd been there with Jerry at our grade school and high school graduations, and I was there with him at his most important graduation, from this life to the next. I'd stood by him as best man at his wedding, as he had at mine. My final tangible act of friendship in this life was to conduct his memorial service, a tear-filled, laughter-filled Christ-centered celebration of his life.

Looking at Jerry's uninhabited body as I sat next to his bed reminded me of what both of us knew and had openly discussed. Death is the dissolving of union between spirit and body. The body dies but the person lives on. Death is not a wall, it's a tunnel. It's not an end, it's a transition.

When Jerry died, the room took on a profound sense of vacancy. His body was a temple in which his spirit and God's had dwelt. The moment he died, the temple lay deserted. "Ichabod"—the glory had departed. Jerry's wasted body was not what was left of him. It was simply what he left. Jerry didn't end. He just relocated. He didn't cease to exist. He just got up and walked out and went where I couldn't see him from here.

When I think of friendships without Christ, it saddens me to realize they're like old clocks, winding down with each tick, destined to ultimately stop, the mainspring forever broken, never to be wound up again. My relationship with Jerry wasn't like that. His death wasn't an end to our friendship. It was only an interruption.

Our time here was the preliminaries, not the main event, the tune-up, not the concert. The friendship that began on earth will resume and thrive and grow in a far better world, the world for which we were made, a world of wonders beyond our wildest dreams. The world where Jerry now lives.

I miss you, Jer. Pick some favorite places we can hang out when I get there, okay? The *real* adventures are still to come, aren't they? I long for the great reunion, old friend.

The Opposite of Boredom

One way to perceive heaven more clearly is to consider how different it is from hell. Let your thoughts be stretched with these portrayals from *Edge of Eternity:*

Heaven: "the exploding universe of life."

Hell: "the imploding pinpoint of death."

Heaven: "cosmic and getting bigger all the time" and "a vast estate in which galaxies are but steppingstones."

Hell: "microscopic and getting smaller all the time" and "smaller than the smallest particle of Earth."

Heaven's inhabitants: "great and ever growing."

Hell's inhabitants: "shrunken and ever shrinking"; "tiny people who were once bigger and could have been magnificent; small and petty people, with nowhere to go, nothing to explore but their own grievances and missed opportunities."

Heaven: where "right choices are forever celebrated."

Hell: where "wrong choices are endlessly reviewed and regretted—especially the choice to refuse the greatest gift ever offered."

Heaven: "a trillion different colors."

Hell: "only the eternal gray."

Heaven: where people "are wonderfully different, united by their differentness."

Hell: where people "are horribly alike, divided by their sameness."

In *Deadline*, "Finney pondered that if the atmosphere of earth was nitrogen and oxygen, and the atmosphere of hell was sulfur and acid, then the atmosphere of heaven was joy and delight."

Every joy on earth—including the joy of reunion—is but an inkling, a whisper of greater Joy. Niagara Falls, Lake Victoria, the Grand Canyon, the world's great mountains and coastlines, all these will prove to be but rough sketches of heaven.

Having seen and painted earth's wonders, now in heaven Dani says, "The best parts of the old world were sneak previews of this one. Like little foretastes, like licking the spoon from Mama's beef stew an hour before supper."

Dani's surprised that she's able to paint in heaven. But why the surprise, her angel asks. God gives gifts and passions to his children on earth. Why would we think he'd withdraw those in heaven? We have every reason to expect him to enhance our gifts and passions, certainly not to diminish them.

Earth leads directly into heaven, just as it leads directly into hell. Life here is a running start into one or the other. Heaven and hell are both retroactive to earth. The best of earth is a glimpse of heaven, the worst of earth a glimpse of hell. Earth is the in-between world touched both by heaven and hell, affording a choice between the two.

The One who by his presence makes heaven heaven, will by his absence make hell hell. Dante's sign that hung over the entrance to hell's inferno is tragically accurate: "Abandon hope all ye who enter here." Hell is heaven refused.

Even among many Bible-believing churches, hell has become the "h-word," seldom talked about anymore. It doesn't even appear in many evangelistic booklets.

We've bought into Satan's lie that it's unloving and uncivilized—even unChristlike—to talk about hell. But the truth is, our Lord Jesus said more about hell than anyone else (e.g. Matthew 10:28; 13:40-42; Mark 9:43). So, either Christ wasn't Christlike, or our perspective is wrong.

Jesus knew what we need to learn—if you love people, you tell them the truth. The most basic truth is there are only two possible eternal destinations, heaven and hell, one just as real as the other. Our default destination is hell—unless and until we bow our knees to Jesus Christ, that's where we're headed. (Notice the modern lie that heaven is the default destination.)

Hell is a place of punishment designed for Satan and the fallen angels (Matthew 25:41,46; Revelation 20:10). However, it will also be inhabited by all who don't accept God's gift of redemption in Christ (Revelation 20:12-15).

Hell is as literal as heaven and as eternal as heaven (Matthew 25:46). In hell people are fully conscious and retain all their capacities and desires with no hope for fulfillment for all eternity (Luke 16:22-31).

God so much wants for us not to go to hell that he paid the

ultimate price so that we wouldn't have to. Nevertheless, apart from trusting Christ for salvation, any person's eternal future will be spent in hell.

"Those who are never thirsty are never refreshed," Torel said. "Those who do not hunger are never filled. That is the beauty of heaven and the horror of hell. For in hell need never dies, but it is never satisfied. Desire never ends, but the ultimate object of every desire is forever absent—Elyon himself."

Hell is called by an angel in *Edge of Eternity*, "the only uninteresting place in the universe." It isn't some giant lounge where between drinks people tell stories of their escapades on earth. It's eternal destruction, separation from God and probably solitary confinement from men as well (2 Thessalonians 1:9).

While there are a number of heaven scenes in both *Deadline* and *Dominion*, I chose to have only one hell scene in each to emphasize the fact that hell has no plot, no developments, no excitement, nothing to anticipate but eternal sameness. Heaven will be the great eternal story, always unfolding. Hell will be but a single footnote. There alone God will withdraw his presence and sin will finally be allowed to do what it does, to suck out all life and meaning. Hence, eternal boredom.

In contrast to hell, "Heaven is the very opposite of boredom," the angelic Zyor tells Finney in *Deadline*.

In heaven we'll be at home with the God who loves us and whom we love—and lovers are never bored with each other. The person who truly loves and belongs to God could never be bored in his presence.

We'll explore and discover God's very being, an experience

delightful beyond comprehension. We'll delight in the richness and diversity of the triune God, understanding more and more clearly the meaning behind his names and attributes. The sense of wonder we see among heaven's inhabitants in Revelation 4–5 suggests an ever-deepening appreciation of God's greatness. This isn't all there is to heaven, but if it was, it would be more than enough.

If you had the opportunity to spend the evening with any person, whether still on earth or in the world next door, who would you choose?

Probably someone fascinating, knowledgeable, and accomplished. High on my list would be people like C. S. Lewis, A.W. Tozer, Francis Schaeffer, Jonathan Edwards, Charles Spurgeon, and Amy Carmichael. Or Jeremiah, Esther, John the Baptist, Mary, and Paul.

Perhaps you'd choose someone beautiful and talented. Maybe you'd hope that at the end of the evening they would have enjoyed your company, too, and would want to spend time with you again.

Well, who is more beautiful, talented, knowledgeable, fascinating, and interesting than Jesus Christ? Is he the person you chose? The good news is, he chose you. If you're a Christian you'll be with him for eternity and enjoy many fascinating dinner conversations. And at the end of the evening you'll know that he enjoyed your company. In fact he paid the ultimate price to build a bridge across the chasm just so he could have you over to his place for eternity.

Do you actually think it could ever be boring to be with *that* person in *that* place?

As a bonus, we'll also get to meet and spend time with all those others on our lists whose home is heaven. Matthew 8:11 says we'll come from all over to have dinner in heaven with Abraham and Isaac and Jacob. We'll meet the others as well. You could spend the evening with your great-great-grandfather or your great-great-granddaughter—or both together. Lack of time and opportunity won't be a problem.

God is an Artist who delights in always designing and creating new things. He's constantly coming up with new ways to display his wonders. Heaven, Zyor explains, is "an endless repository of wealth, a continuous succession of adventures to benefit and delight his children."

Art is a reflection of the artist. Because God is endlessly creative and fascinating, heaven—his magnum opus—will be too.

Will we learn in heaven? Yes! Ephesians 2:6-7 says, "God raised us up with Christ and seated us with him in the heavenly realms in Christ Jesus, in order that in the coming ages he might show the incomparable riches of his grace." The word "show" means to reveal, in a progressive ongoing way. When we die we'll know a lot more than we do now, but we won't know all we'll ever know. In heaven we'll learn new things about God, we'll go ever-deeper in our understanding.

God is infinite and inexhaustible (Isaiah 55:9). We'll never comprehend all there is to know about him. But we're told we should be always "growing in the knowledge of God" (Colossians 1:10). Since we'll still be finite and he'll still be infinite, that will continue in heaven.

David's longing was to live in God's house "to behold the

beauty of the LORD, and to inquire in his temple" (Psalm 27:4, KJV). "Inquire" is a word that suggests seeking, studying, questioning, probing in our understanding and worship. When it comes to God, there will always be more to inquire of, ask about, discuss, explore, and discover. Teaching? Research? Writing? Reading? Yes, presumably. Why not?

There will be *process* in heaven, a continual progression of stimulating discoveries and fresh learning, as we keep grasping more of God. Since we'll be learning about him, presumably we'll be learning more about his saints, angelic beings, and all his creation. (Think of the wonders of this present cosmos—how much greater will the new ones be?) The realization that we'll never stop learning in heaven really excites me.

Perhaps God will allow us to go back in time and observe the events of earth as they happened. Since earth's history has been the stage for the King's great drama, we may well become students of history, not from a distance, but up close. Maybe we'll take exploratory "field trips" together. Why not?

Since angels, also finite and already in heaven, long to grow in their understanding (1 Peter 1:12), shouldn't we expect to do the same? God himself will be our teacher—and likely angels and saints will be our mentors.

For this process to occur, it seems to require a framework of *time* in heaven. People often ask, "But doesn't the Bible say 'and time shall be no more'?" The answer is, no it doesn't—that phrase is from a hymn, not the Bible. Timelessness, I think, is another one of those myths about heaven that makes us think of it as unreal and unnatural. "With the Lord a day is like a thousand years, and a thousand years are like a day" (2 Peter 3:8). This says God is timeless; it does not say *we* will be.

Revelation shows heaven's inhabitants operating within time. The descriptions include successive actions, such as falling down at God's throne and casting crowns before him. There's a natural sequence of events—things occur one after the another.

Beings in heaven enter into sequential moments on earth, right down to rejoicing over conversions as they happen (Luke 15:7,10). They even anticipate specific events they ask God to bring about on earth (Revelation 6:9-11). Repeatedly, we see heaven's seamless interaction with successive events occurring on earth.

In the new heavens and earth, the tree of life is described as "yielding its fruit every month" (Revelation 22:2). Revelation 8:1 speaks of "silence in heaven for about half an hour." What could be a clearer indication that time can be measured in heaven than references to "every month" and "half an hour"?

Even the presence of music in heaven demands time, doesn't it? Meter, tempo, and rests are all essential components of music...and each is time-related. Songs begin and end.

We are finite creatures. Just as we're limited to the realm of space, we're limited to the realm of time. God alone is infinite. Time is the habitation of creatures. Only the Creator is exempt from it. Yet he chooses to enter into time that he may communicate and experience life with his creatures.

We'll have all eternity to keep exploring the fascinating and unending story of heaven.

In *The Chronicles of Narnia*, C. S. Lewis paints a beautiful picture of heaven in the final book, *The Last Battle*. The book begins with a near collision of a railroad train, where the children are thrust into Narnia. But when their adventure is over, the children are afraid they will be sent back to earth again.

Having experienced the joys and wonders of Narnia and the presence of Aslan—the Lion who is Christ—the thought of returning to earth was unbearable. Then, in the final section, (called "Farewell to the Shadow-Lands") Aslan, the great Lion, gives the children some good news:

> "There *was* a real railway accident," said Aslan softly. "Your father and mother and all of you are, as you used to call it in the Shadow-Lands, dead. The term is over: the holidays have begun. The dream is ended: this is the morning."
>
> And as He spoke He no longer looked to them like a lion; but the things that began to happen after that were so great and beautiful that I cannot write them. And for us this is the end of all the stories, and we can most truly say that they all lived happily ever after. But for them it was only the beginning of the real story. All their life in this world and all their adventures in Narnia had only been the cover and the title page. Now at last they were beginning Chapter One of the Great Story, which no one on earth has read; which goes on for ever; in which every chapter is better than the one before.

Thirteen

Will We Remember Our Lives on Earth?

In the spring of 1991, my friend Steve Keels and I went with two missionaries to the Soviet Union shortly before its collapse.

Lenin had promised a thousand-year reign of communism and the death of Christianity. Now, after seventy years, the people were sick of the hollow misery this pseudo-Messiah had brought them. On "Lenin's Day"—his birthday—in the Ukrainian city of Kamanets-Podolsky, we did something we were told had never been done there. We went into the public schools and shared the gospel in ten different classrooms, then passed out Bibles to every student, teacher, and principal. All accepted them with wide eyes. Most had never seen a Bible. Steve and I were amazed.

In all those classrooms huge pictures of Lenin peered down on us, disapproving but helpless, while Soviet children—including the communist youth with their red kerchiefs—listened intently as we shared the gospel of Christ.

Whenever I remember that trip, a flood of stories rushes into my mind. There was Sergei, on the train from Moscow, whom we gave an illustrated New Testament. He devoured it. Before we arrived in Kiev he and his brother came to Christ.

We spoke at a rally in an auditorium that formerly had been open only to card-carrying members of the Communist party. A month earlier, however, the *Jesus Film* had been shown there. The effect had been electric, and we came in on its coattails. Thousands attended the rally. Many came forward to receive Christ. Hundreds pressed forward asking for Bibles. A sea of humanity, eyes longing for something more, reached out for God's Word.

Everywhere we went they pumped us with questions about the Bible, Christ, heaven, and hell. After a powerful service in which many came to Christ, we sat in the church basement. Suddenly in walked a young Asian-looking man, weary and worn from long travel. No one recognized him. As he explained who he was, they translated his story to us. He was from a remote part of Siberia, where his church had heard that Bibles had come into the USSR somewhere near the city of Kiev. His church had no Bibles, so they collected as much money as they could, laid hands on him, and sent him forth as their ambassador to search for God's Word.

This young man had traveled seven days on a boat from his village—where the only land travel was by dogsled—to the nearest city with an airport. From there he traveled by plane, train, and bus in search of Scriptures. But after traveling twenty-six hundred miles, he still hadn't found a single Bible to take home with him. The Lord led him to this church where we had just delivered a shipment of Bibles. The brothers of the Ukrainian church gave him some of their precious Bibles to take back to his people.

We visited a children's hospital. The chief doctor and administrator was a communist of great status. He invited us to speak, and for over an hour our missionary friend, Bill, shared the gospel with sixty doctors, nurses, and hospital support staff.

This physician invited us to his home for dinner. Before we arrived, one of the local pastors, who was coming with us, told us, "This is an historic event in our city. Never before has a man of such high standing, and a communist, invited Christians to eat with him in his home. They have always persecuted us." He seemed very nervous.

We had a delightful dinner, served by the physician's wife, herself a prominent doctor. After dinner we presented the doctor's wife with a special gift, a children's Bible in Russian. Suddenly tears welled up in her eyes and she said something. Someone translated. She'd said, "For many years I have dreamed that some-day I would hold in my hands a Bible." She added, with awe in her voice, "I will read it to my granddaughter."

I relate these events not only to tell of God's great work on earth, but to provide a context for asking a question: When Steve and I get to heaven, will we remember these things we saw on earth? Will these memories that are so precious to us now go up in smoke when we enter heaven? Will the God-starved people of the Soviet Union forget the mighty wind of the Spirit that swept across that land in those days?

Will I forget coming to Christ, marrying my wife, baptizing my daughters? Will I forget how God used trials in my life to make me more Christlike? Will I forget the way he provided for me every day, the strength he gave, the things and people he sent to make me laugh and cry? I see absolutely no biblical reason why

I would not remember these things. I see every reason why I would.

One qualification is in order. I've heard people say, "We can't understand that now, but we'll understand in heaven, because then we'll know everything." In heaven, we'll see and know clearly (1 Corinthians 13:12), with far greater understanding than we have now. However, the notion that "we'll know everything in heaven" is certainly wrong. If we did know everything, we'd be God. He alone is infinite and all-knowing. We will always be finite, even after we become glorified in heaven. The angels in heaven don't know everything (Mark 13:32). Neither will we.

But while some attribute too much knowledge to people in heaven, most attribute far too little. Hence, this popular myth that in heaven we'll have no remembrance of our lives on earth. For some reason—in some cases, it may be wishful thinking—we disassociate our existence on earth from our future existence. But God sees a direct connection between them. Your life on earth has *eternal* significance. It has been recorded in the sight of all heaven and will serve as an ongoing reference point for your eternal future.

This concept of remembering our earthly past once we're in heaven seems to be controversial. So let's examine it closely.

We're told that after we die we'll give an account of our lives on earth, down to specific actions and words (2 Corinthians 5:10; Matthew 12:36). Obviously, we *must* remember the things we've done on earth—how else could we give an account of them? In fact, considering our improved minds and clear thinking, our memories of our earthly past should be more acute, not less. We won't remember less of earth, but more.

Our specific acts of faithfulness on earth will survive the fire of judgment and be brought into heaven with us (1 Corinthians 3:14). We're told that in heaven the wedding dress worn by the bride of Christ "stands for the righteous acts of the saints" done on earth (Revelation 19:7-8). The very clothes we'll wear testify to what we did on earth. (Let's be sure we're fully clothed!) These righteous deeds done on earth are said to "follow" us to heaven (Revelation 14:13).

The positions of authority and the treasures awarded in heaven to the faithful will perpetually remind heaven's inhabitants—including us—of the lives we lived on earth. That, after all, is what the rewards are given for (Matthew 6:19-21; 19:21; Luke 12:33; 19:17,19; 1 Timothy 6:19; Revelation 2:26-28).

God makes a record in heaven of what everyone—both nonbelievers and believers—does on earth. We know that this record outlasts a person's life here. For the believer it lasts at least until he stands before the judgment seat of Christ (2 Corinthians 5:10). For the unbeliever it lasts at least right up to the Great White Throne judgment (Revelation 20:11-13). In fact, it lasts into hell, since the rich man in hell remembered his earthly life, including his brothers and Lazarus (Luke 16:27-31). He even recognized Abraham across the great gulf.

Will I forget about Sergei coming to Christ on the train? Will Sergei forget how God changed his life that day? Will my friends and I ever forget the tears streaming down the face of the communist woman grasping the Bible? Will we ever forget going to ten Russian classrooms where the gospel was shared for the first time? Isn't the twenty-six-hundred-mile journey of a young Siberian man sent by a Bibleless church in search of God's Word the stuff of which heaven's stories will be made?

The martyrs in heaven mentioned in Revelation 6:9-11 clearly remember what happened on earth, including the great suffering they underwent. With strong emotion they anticipate and look forward to God's coming judgment. This passage argues against the prevalent belief that to remember any unpleasant things would automatically strip us of happiness in heaven. Heaven's joy is not dependent upon an erased mind, but a renewed mind. That will include a sense of the relative greatness of the eternal joys of heaven in comparison to the brevity of our earthly sufferings (Romans 8:18).

Malachi 3:16 speaks of "a scroll of remembrance" written in God's presence "concerning those who feared the LORD and honored his name." In the world of biblical times, such documents typically were recorded by the king's scribes and periodically read in his presence to ensure that worthy actions done by his subjects would be remembered and properly rewarded (Esther 6:1-11). The scroll mentioned in Malachi may be recorded in heaven by angels acting as God's scribes.

Since we're told that this scroll exists, it's hard to envision the God of history later destroying it or everyone in heaven ignoring it in the ages to come. It seems more likely that these records of the faithful works of God's people on earth will be periodically read (perhaps viewed as they actually happened) in heaven throughout the ages. They will be rejoiced over by God, his angels, and ourselves.

The young man from Siberia will be on those scrolls—I'm sure of it. I look forward to seeing the end of the story, which I still do not know—what happened on his journey home and the response of his church when they saw the Word of God for the very first time.

Forget earth once we're in heaven? This assumption betrays an unbiblical belief—that our lives here are insignificant and have no real bearing on eternity.

Nothing could be further from the truth.

Just What Will We Remember and Forget?

Remember the youth pastor's wife who was told by her Christian teacher that when she got to heaven she wouldn't know anyone or anything from earth? For many years this terrified her. Does the Bible suggest any such thing?

In addition to the scriptural evidence laid out in the previous chapter, consider the fact that memory is a basic element of personality. Since it will truly be *us* in heaven, there must be some continuity of memory from here to there. Heaven will cleanse us of sin and error, but it won't erase our lives and memories. The people we've known here, who God has sent to impact our lives, are his gift to us, as we are his gift to them. To forget these people would be to forget God's grace and provision. It's unthinkable. There is no biblical basis whatsoever for this belief.

The lessons we've learned on earth about God's love and grace and justice surely will not be lost, but will carry over to heaven. They'll be built upon and greatly expanded, yes, but not replaced or eliminated. There seems every reason to believe that just as our earthly works done for Christ will survive this life and be brought into the next (1 Corinthians 3:13-14), so will our Christ-centered experiences and relationships.

Since none of us will have learned everything on earth God desires us to, once we're in heaven perhaps we will review our lives on earth and this time take a firm hold of every lesson he intended. That could help our remembrance of our past to be not an experience of regret, but of gratitude.

One verse is often cited as proof that we will not be able to remember our lives on earth. Isaiah 65:17 says, "Behold, I will create new heavens and a new earth. The former things will not be remembered, nor will they come to mind." What's the meaning of this verse?

First, it must be weighed against dozens of other passages of Scripture. For instance, in the heavenly city the gates have inscribed on them the names of the twelve tribes and the apostles (Revelation 21:12-14). This is obviously a memorial. The whole point of a memorial is to cause us to remember. We will remember the twelve tribes and the apostles, who they were and what they did *on earth*.

Every believer's crowns and rewards will continuously remind heaven's inhabitants of acts of faithfulness to God done on earth. Consider Christ's nail-scarred hands and feet in his eternal resurrection body (John 20:24-29). Don't they prove his suffering and works on earth—and our sin, which necessitated them—will *not* be forgotten? Whatever the "former things" of Isaiah 65:17 are, there's a great deal they cannot include.

The key to what Isaiah 65:17 actually means, as usual, is context. It flows directly from the previous verse: "For the past troubles will be forgotten and hidden from my eyes." The primary party doing the "forgetting" is God. This doesn't suggest literal lack of memory, as if the omniscient God couldn't recall the past. God knows everything. Rather, it's like God saying, "I... will remember their sins no more" (Jeremiah 31:34). It means he will choose not to call to mind or to hold against us our past sins.

We can forget in the same sense. If someone does a wrong against me and I say, "Forget it," or "I'm not going to remember that," what I mean is not that the data will be erased from my brain, but I won't dwell on it or hold it against someone.

In eternity, past sins and sufferings won't plague us, nor interfere with God's acceptance of us. We won't dwell on them. Likewise, we'll be capable of choosing not to recall our past troubles and sorrows in any way that would diminish heaven.

A woman once plagued by nightmares of an evil man who abused her will have the capacity not to remember him, not to be haunted by what he did to her. She will not relive the horror—but she will remember the faithfulness of God and perhaps see for the first time the actions of God and angels done on her behalf. She will also understand something we presently cannot—why he allowed it to happen.

Joseph saw in his lifetime why God allowed his brothers to sell him into slavery, something that had to be horribly frightening to a boy. He told them, "You intended to harm me, but God intended it for good" (Genesis 50:20).

I've had difficult things happen to me, in which I already see clearly the sovereign purposes of God. This includes a multi-million dollar court judgment against me for peaceful pro-life intervention at abortion clinics. It includes having many people criticize and misunderstand, and having to step away from a pastoral ministry I loved, so those who kill children for a living couldn't take money from me or my church. It includes becoming an insulin-dependent diabetic, requiring multiple shots and blood tests every day, and losing to death a number of loved ones.

I wouldn't want to forget any of these, and already I can clearly see God's hand at work in all of them. There are other things I don't understand, but eventually I will. And once we understand God's purposes in something, why would we *want* to forget it? I look forward not to forgetting the hard times on earth, but seeing them with eternal perspective.

A Ukrainian pastor told me, "I was trained for pastoral ministry by seventeen years in Siberian Seminary." At first, I didn't get it, but then it hit me. "Siberian Seminary" was his euphemism for the cold hard Siberian labor camps to which many pastors were banished for obeying God and disobeying the communist government. They called it seminary because there they learned to follow Christ, to serve the church, to build their lives not on present circumstances but on eternal realities. I have no doubt they learned far more at their seminary than I did at mine.

Even while on earth, this pastor treasured the memories of God's faithfulness and the lessons he learned in prison. How much more will he appreciate those memories when he ponders them in heaven?

Recalling our earthly troubles and sorrows would not depress us, but deepen the joys of heaven, as darkness brings out the glory of light. This contrast would be lost if our former sorrows and sinful state were literally forgotten.

While God will wipe away the tears and sorrow attached to this world, the drama of God's work in human history will *not* be erased from our minds. We won't forget about Joseph and Jeremiah, about the martyrs who suffered for their Lord. I won't forget about those who loved me, about my wife's sacrifices for me, about my children's acts of faithfulness for Christ.

I won't forget the Hungarian pastors I met with secretly behind the Iron Curtain, or the Russian brother who told me how he grew up attending church, year after year, under his mother's skirt, because the KGB would arrest people who brought their children to church. I won't forget the Chinese, Cambodian, and African believers whose lives touched me so deeply. In fact their faces will be some of the first I look for in heaven.

"But surely we'll forget our sin." Will we? Obviously we won't be plagued by it. But if we ever forget who we once were and what we once did, how could we appreciate the depth and meaning of Christ's love and sacrifice for us? How could we worship Christ for his amazing grace if we forget our utter rebellion and unworthiness that make his grace so amazing (Romans 5:6-8)?

Heaven's happiness will not be dependent on our ignorance of what happened on earth. Rather, it will be enhanced by our awareness of God's grace and justice in the unfolding drama of redemption performed on that stage called earth...a drama in which we each played a part we will always remember. A drama in which the Playwright and Director's purposes will at last be clear.

Let me propose one more thought that many find hard to accept. I'm confident that in heaven we'll pray to God, and it's likely we'll intercede for those still on earth. Consider the evidence.

We know that Christ, the God-man, is in heaven interceding for people here (Romans 8:34). He's a man who has died and gone to heaven and is now praying for those on earth.

Then in Revelation 6:10 we see martyrs in heaven praying to God, asking him to take specific action on earth. These are saints who have died and are now in God's presence. They're actively praying for God's justice on earth for persecuted believers. It seems likely they'd also be interceding for other aspects of their suffering brethren's welfare. (Their keen urgency about the justice of God demonstrates again we won't be passive in heaven—we'll be far less tolerant of persecution and a hundred other evils.)

The saints in heaven are just as much a part of the body of Christ as the saints on earth. (Ephesians 3:15 speaks of "his whole family in heaven and on earth.") Their sense of connection and loyalty to their brethren logically would be enhanced in heaven, not diminished, wouldn't it?

There's no indication in Scripture that we should pray for the dead. It would do no good to pray for them, since "man is destined to die once and, after that to face judgment" (Hebrews 9:27). Once they die, there's nothing that can be done to change the state of a believer or unbeliever.

The pertinent question is not "Should we pray for the dead?" but "Do the dead pray for us?" Revelation 5:8 speaks of the "prayers of the saints" in a context that could include the saints in heaven. Prayer is simply talking to God. Angels talk to God, therefore angels pray. We will communicate with God in heaven. That means we'll pray in heaven. Will we pray less or more? Given our enhanced righteousness, it seems that in heaven our prayers would be all the more frequent as well as more "powerful and effective" (James 5:16).

If people in heaven witness some of what transpires on earth—and as we've seen, they clearly can—then it would seem strange for them not to intercede for those they observe.

It all boils down to assumptions. If we assume those in heaven aren't interested in earth—and they don't observe or feel connected with people on earth—then we'll conclude they aren't praying for us. If, on the other hand, we assume saints in heaven observe and take interest in God's program and people on earth, it stands to reason they would be interceding for their comrades still on the battlefield.

Since God and the angels are clearly concerned with earth, shouldn't saints in heaven be? And since heaven is a place where saints talk to God, shouldn't we assume that once we're in heaven we'll pray to God for those on earth?

Why wouldn't we?

Fifteen

Can Those in Heaven See What Happens Here?

Another controversial concept I've already alluded to and built into my novels is that in heaven we'll be aware of at least some of what's happening on earth. This, too, is confirmed by a look at Scripture.

When Babylon is destroyed in Revelation 18, an angel points to the events happening on earth and says, "Rejoice over her, O heaven! Rejoice, saints and apostles and prophets! God has judged her for the way she treated you" (18:20). Since the angel specifically addresses people in heaven, the implication is that they're watching and listening to what is happening below. At the very least, they're being told about it.

In the next chapter, we read about "the roar of a great multitude in heaven shouting: 'Hallelujah'" and praising God for the specific events of judgment that have just taken place (Revelation 19:1-5). Again, the saints in heaven are responding to what's happening on earth.

Then we read of heaven's armies returning with Christ to set up his millennial kingdom (19:11-14). It seems unthinkable these soldiers would be in the dark about the culmination of history about to take place on earth. God and his angels and they themselves (Revelation 17:14) are about to march to the ultimate battle in the history of the universe, after which Christ will be crowned king. This is not a situation into which someone walks unaware.

Earth is like center court at Wimbledon—all eyes are on it. If in heaven we'll be concerned with what God is concerned with, and if his interest is in the spiritual battle on earth, why would we *not* be watching his works here with intense interest? If the Sovereign God's attentions are toward earth, why wouldn't those of his heavenly subjects be also? When a great war is transpiring, are soldiers in the Commander's service uninformed and unaware of it, blissfully taking strolls and picking daisies?

In the Old Testament, when Samuel was brought back to earth from heaven, he was aware of what King Saul had been doing and had failed to do (1 Samuel 28:18).

When Moses and Elijah were sent from heaven to the transfiguration of Christ on earth, they talked with Jesus about his approaching death in Jerusalem (Luke 9:31). They were clearly aware of the earthly events they'd stepped into.

Hebrews 12:1 tells us to "run with perseverance the race marked out for us" and creates the mental picture of a "great cloud of witnesses" watching us. These witnesses are the saints who've gone before us. The imagery suggests that those saints, the spiritual "athletes" of old, are now watching us and cheering us on from the stands of heaven. They're said not merely to have preceded us, but to "surround" us. Each day, each moment, a million eyes are watching us. (Depending on what we're doing, this thought can cause either dread or great comfort and inspiration.)

Angels observed Christ on earth (1 Timothy 3:16), and they know what's happening here (Luke 1:26-28; 1 Corinthians 11:10). If angels in heaven know what's going on, why not saints? Don't the people of God who are in heaven have as much vested interests in the events on earth as angels do? In fact, don't they have more?

Jesus said, "There will be more rejoicing in heaven over one sinner who repents than over ninety-nine...who do not need to" (Luke 15:7), and, "There is rejoicing in the presence of the angels of God over one sinner who repents" (15:10). Who besides God himself is doing this rejoicing in heaven in the presence of angels? Doesn't it logically include the saints in heaven, who would most appreciate the joy and wonder of human conversion? To rejoice over these conversions requires they be aware of earthly events.

Despite such clear scriptural evidence, some still insist that people in heaven are unconcerned with and unaware of what's happening on earth. I believe this is mainly due to a deduction based on one faulty premise: For people to be happy in heaven, they can't know what's happening on earth. That argument is worth taking a closer look at.

"It wouldn't be heaven," people say, "if we knew of bad things happening on earth, since we're promised there will be no more crying or pain in heaven."

But we have to remember that heaven is still heaven for God—and he knows exactly what's happening on earth.

Heaven is still heaven for the angels, who also know what's

happening on earth. Angels in heaven can even see the torment of hell (Revelation 14:10), but it doesn't minimize heaven.

A particularly interesting passage is Luke 16:19-31, the account Jesus gave of Lazarus and the rich man at whose gate he begged. Subsequent to their deaths, we find the two men in the afterlife. Lazarus is at Abraham's side, and from there, in Paradise, both Lazarus and Abraham can see the rich man's agonies in hell.

Notice that this awareness of hell did not in any way cause Paradise to cease to be Paradise for Lazarus and Abraham. If people in heaven could see into hell without ruining heaven, surely nothing they could see on earth could ruin it. Hell cannot trump or negate heaven; neither can earth.

Abraham speaks of a chasm that those in heaven and hell can't cross, but which they can see across into the other place. If this is true of heaven and hell, doesn't it seem likely it might be true of heaven and earth? Could there be a separation between earth and heaven that prevents direct intervention but still allows those in heaven to see what's happening on earth?

We must also remember that the promise of no more crying is made after the end of the world, after the Great White Throne judgment, and after "the old order of things has passed away" when there is no more suffering on earth (Revelation 21:1-4). We'll no longer cry then because there'll be nothing left to cry about. This passage is an argument not for tearlessness in the present heaven, but for tearlessness in the new heaven and new earth.

Certainly the people in heaven are not frail beings whose joy can be maintained only if they're kept ignorant of what's really going on elsewhere. In fact, even if such knowledge in heaven did produce some sadness, the old order hasn't yet passed away and sadness may still be appropriate. Heaven is not in its final state.

While on earth, Christ grieved for people (Matthew 23:37-39; John 11:33-36). Is he no longer capable of grieving because he's in heaven? Or does he still hurt for his people when they suffer? Acts 9:4-5 seems to give a clear answer—Jesus is in heaven but tells Saul that by persecuting Christians he has been persecuting *him*. Think about it—Christ is in heaven, yet is suffering along with his people on earth. If Christ can hurt for his people while in heaven, couldn't we do the same?

Going into the heavenly presence of Christ surely won't make us less compassionate, but more. Even with the predominant joy that already exists in heaven, in light of the fact that there's still so much evil and pain on earth, believers in heaven may periodically experience sadness until the evil and pain are permanently gone. That may not fit with what we've always believed about heaven. But the relevant question is, does it fit with what Scripture actually tells us?

In fact, in some metaphysical way Christians on earth are already linked both to Christ and to heaven (Ephesians 2:6). As Christ is in us, heaven is in us even now, and a part of us is in heaven with Christ. The lines of distinction we draw strictly disconnecting earth and heaven are not true to God's Word!

Our awareness in heaven of the reality of earthly trouble and sorrow and sin—both past and present—could set a sharp contrast to heaven's glory and light. Maybe an awareness of the perfect justice of hell will enhance the depth of gratitude to God among those in heaven.

As for the events of this life that are so terrible, consider what happens to Nick Seagrave in *Edge of Eternity*:

> A vast fabric stretched across the sky. Bending back my head, I saw on the fabric countless unsightly lumps and knots, like thick, rough yarn with frayed strings.
>
> Suddenly, Marcus beside me, I was yanked up into the sky and pulled through a hole in the center of the fabric. Now I was on the other side, the topside. I looked down and saw a beautiful work of art, like needlepoint or cross-stitching, a magnificent tapestry. The yarn and threads had been perfectly knitted together in elaborate design by the hands of a master craftsman. I saw in the center of the tapestry the Woodsman on a tree. I saw how a senseless murder, history's worst act of betrayal, was the centerpiece of a glorious design. Surrounding it I saw other tragedies, absurd and incomprehensible events that now had clear meaning and purpose.
>
> "It's stunning," I said to Marcus. "Before I saw only the underside, the ugly knots and frays. I never saw the design, the beauty."
>
> "No wonder," Marcus said. "Until now, you have always lived on the wrong side of the tapestry."

Our happiness in heaven will not be based on our failure to know what's happening on earth. Rather, it will be based on our being with Christ and seeing with new eyes.

The joys of heaven are not rooted in ignorance. They're rooted in perspective.

Sixteen

A Greater Miracle

When Nick's companions in *Edge of Eternity* finally pass through the gates of the City of Light, their responses may mirror ours when we enter our long tomorrow:

"This is it…the country for which I was made!"

"At last, the real world!"

"I've been born. All my life on Earth was but a series of labor pains preparing me for this."

"This is joy itself. Every foretaste of joy in the Shadowlands was but the stab, the pang, the inconsolable longing for this place!"

"How could anyone be satisfied with less than this?"

The moment we enter heaven, we'll know it's exactly where we belong.

But there's something that still stands between us and heaven. Unless the Lord returns for us in our lifetimes, before we experience heaven, we must go through a doorway from our short today to our long tomorrow.

That doorway is *death.*

Death is life's greatest certainty. Death will come whether or not you're prepared. But death is not an end; it's a transition that will bring us face to face with our Creator.

The Bible calls death "the last enemy" (1 Corinthians 15:26). It's our ultimate problem. God sent his Son to defeat this enemy, to solve the problem. But we must accept his solution while we're still in this world. We must reach out our hand and take from him the ticket he offers us before we can get on the train—or before the train leaves without us. The absolute certainty of our death gives the gospel its urgency.

Let me tell you about a self-made man, fiercely independent. He fended for himself in the Great Depression, learning to do everything his way and not to trust anyone. He was more resistant to the gospel than any person I've ever known.

He was my dad.

A year after I became a Christian at age fifteen, my mom came to the Lord, but my father dug in his heels. He told me never to talk to him again about that "religious stuff."

I gave him copies of books I wrote. I always included the gospel in them, knowing they were the only Christian books he'd read. Some of what I said in my novels was there just for my Dad.

Through the years, Mom and I continued praying for him. After Mom died, he moved across the river to Vancouver, Washington. Then, at age eighty-four, he was diagnosed with terminal cancer. The doctor said he had six months to live.

One day, several months after the diagnosis, I received a call. The moment I picked up the phone I knew something was terribly wrong. Dad sounded extremely distressed. "I've called to say good-bye," he told me. He said he was in pain from the cancer, and he knew the end was coming. He didn't want an agonizing death.

"I've got a gun to my head," he added. "Sorry to leave you a mess."

I knew my Dad well enough to know he wasn't bluffing. He'd never bluffed. I begged him to put down the gun and hold on till I got there. I jumped in the car and made the thirty-minute drive in twenty.

I pulled up to the curb, bouncing the tires off it, and jumped out of the car. I knocked on his front door. No answer.

I turned the unlocked knob, walked in, and saw on the living room floor a rifle and a handgun. I called out for my father. No answer. I knew he had other guns in his bedroom.

Holding my breath for what I was about to see, I turned the corner into his bedroom. As I did, Dad walked out and bumped into me.

Heart racing, I hugged him and rushed him to the hospital. After examining him, the doctors scheduled surgery for the next morning.

I came into his hospital room an hour before surgery. I'd prayed that somehow, in his pain, with no easy way out, God would break through to my father.

I opened my Bible to Romans 3. "All have sinned and fall short of the glory of God." My tavern-owning father had been offended at the idea of being called a sinner, so part of me wanted to gloss over this and move quickly past the bad news to the good news.

But I told myself that if I really loved Dad I had to tell him the whole truth. If God was going to do the miracle of conversion, that was his job. Mine was to tell Dad the truth. And nothing could do that better than the Bible itself.

I turned to Romans 6:23—"For the wages of sin is death, but the gift of God is eternal life in Christ Jesus our Lord." Then on to Romans 10:9-10.

After thirty minutes of reading Scripture, I looked at Dad and asked, "Have you ever confessed your sins and asked Jesus Christ to forgive you?" Of course, I knew the answer.

"No…," he acknowledged, then paused for what seemed a long time. During the pause I was already thanking God for this opportunity, certain Dad wouldn't respond but grateful I could console myself at least he'd been given one last chance. Finally he finished his sentence, "…but I think it's about time I did."

Shocked, I said I would pray first, then he could follow. I prayed aloud that God would help Dad to ask him what he wanted to.

When I finished praying, Dad said, "I'm not very good at this." As far as I know he'd never prayed out loud in his life—I'd certainly never heard him.

"That's all right, Dad, God doesn't care about that. He just cares about your heart. Say whatever you want to."

With earnestness and clarity of thought, Dad prayed (I wrote it down), "God, I know that I'm a sinner. I believe Jesus is the Son of God. I ask you to accept me into heaven when I die, so I can be with you and your saints."

I then read many passages of Scripture to him of God's promises of eternal life.

I also read to him Revelation 21:1-7, telling him how I had read it every day to Mom in the last month before she died.

I told Dad that I—as well as Nanci, Karina, and Angela—

105

had prayed many years that he'd come to Christ. "Now we know," I said, "that you'll be with the Lord and Mom and us for eternity."

His face said it all—eyes watering and a peace I'd never seen in him.

The prayers of so many people—beginning with my mother and me twenty-two years earlier—had finally come to fruition. To have prayed so long for a miracle and now to see it actually happen was truly amazing.

At the doors of the surgery unit, I held Dad's hand and thanked God he'd come to know him and had the assurance of eternal life. I prayed for the surgery, but above all I thanked him that Dad was now at peace with God.

The surgery was successful. The next day, I wrote down my feelings in a prayer:

Thank you, my heavenly Father, for a miracle far greater than parting the Red Sea—for bringing my dad to yourself. Thank you for sending your Holy Spirit to ride the crest of the waves of the faithful prayers of your saints all these years.

Thank you for the crushing blow to the evil one, who has been robbed of the pleasure of seeing the eternal destruction of this one created in your image.

And thank you for this kindness to me, my mother, and my family. Had you done nothing else for me, this alone would fill my heart with praise to you for all eternity.

Thank you, my Father and my Friend,
Randy

God gave me five more years with Dad (so much for the six months the doctor predicted) before taking him home, with my wife and daughters and brother and me right there next to him. We tearfully said good-bye, knowing we'd see him again. The moment I'd dreaded all those years—my father's death—was now a moment of pain eclipsed by joy.

As I reflect back on that morning before he went into surgery, I know the worst thing I could have done to my father was to hold back part of God's truth. For without the bad news, there is no good news. Without the truth of God's holiness and the truth of our sin, Christ's work on our behalf becomes meaningless or irrelevant. Without the reality of the hell we deserve, we cannot appreciate the heaven we've been offered.

Without knowing that truth, it's impossible to experience the grace of God. For his grace is not simply kindness—it's a specific response to sin. If there is no knowledge of sin and hell, there can be no experience of the miracle of grace and heaven.

It's God's grace in Christ that takes us through the doorway of death and into the joy of our long tomorrow. There, for the first time, we will be with the Person for whom we were made, in the place for which we were made.

And my dad will be there too.

Stones from the Riverbeds

Midway through *Edge of Eternity*, Nick and his fellow travelers are met by the King's messenger. She gives them burlap sacks and instructions to fill them with stones from the riverbeds they'll cross at night. Then she leaves them with the cryptic words, "In the morning you will be both glad and sad."

But in the morning, they're unable to open their bags and see what's inside. In fact, throughout the journey they're only able to open the bags at night when and if they choose to add more stones.

Nick is reluctant to follow these apparently senseless instructions. Isn't the added weight of these worthless rocks just an unnecessary burden for a weary traveler?

Later, as they finally near the City, they're met again by the messenger and told to present their gifts to the King.

"Gifts?" the travelers ask.

"Yes. The stones you picked up in the riverbeds."

My heart pounded. I put down my worn sack, just over half-full. I pulled out a stone. It glimmered in the sunlight.

"It's gold!" I said. I reached back into the sack. "Silver! A ruby. Look—two diamonds. An emerald! And this one…I've never seen anything like it!"

Vaguely aware of the others shouting. I looked up to see them rifling through their bags, holding up precious stones in the rosy sunlight.

I reached farther into my bag and found what I'd thought were some light stones. I pulled them out and stared at them.

"They're not stones at all," I said. "They're just crumpled balls of straw."

I turned the bag upside down. One last gem fell out, a small one. The rest was straw and stubble.

The contents from Nick's sack are then placed on a grate above a raging bonfire.

The fire immediately consumed the straw, while it burned off impurities from the gold and silver and gems. They glowed with an otherworldly beauty, and I stared at them breathlessly, held captive by their radiance.

Nick then sees the stones from his companions' sacks. From one he sees "dozens of precious gems, perhaps twenty diamonds and chunks of gold and silver." Another companion, whom Nick has thought of as dull-witted, had filled and carried two sacks in his journey. "Here he was," Nick discovers, "with three times as many precious stones as I."

Then everyone watches as their oldest companion Shad, a man whose single-minded pursuit of God often irritated Nick, empties his several sacks to have their precious contents purified in the blaze.

I stared at all those stones. How could one old man have carried them all on our journey? In his own strength it would have been impossible—of course, that was it. He'd carried them with the strength of another.

An angel's voice whispers to Nick: "Choice and consequences. What is done in one world has profound effects on the next."

Then they observe the angel beginning to forge their fire-refined stones into crowns. "You will cast these at the King's feet," the travelers are told.

"And sometimes you will wear them. The King and all the citizens of Charis will be forever reminded of your faithful service. You will remember the meaning of every stone, and so will he. Elyon's book says, 'A scroll of remembrance was written in his presence concerning those who feared the King and honored his name.' All your works are recorded here—every cup of cold water given in his name."

Nick stares at his gemstones and sees animated images within each of them. Pictures that portray each of his prayers and other good deeds—some long-forgotten—done in service to the King.

Finally he understands those cryptic words of the King's messenger.

> The long night was over, and morning was here at last. I looked at the stones I'd picked up, knowing they were my tribute to the King. Seeing them, I'd never felt so glad.
>
> Then I thought about all the stones within my reach, all those I could have picked up but didn't.
>
> I'd never felt so sad.

The five-hundred-year-old play *Everyman* is a picture of all people. As Everyman faces Death he looks among his friends for a companion. Only one friend would accompany him to the other side. His name was "Good Deeds."

This picture is explicitly biblical. Of those who die in the Lord it's said, "their deeds will follow them" (Revelation 14:13). We can't take anything to heaven with us except the things we've done on earth for the good of others and the glory of our Lord.

In Revelation 19:7-8 we're told, "The wedding of the Lamb has come, and his bride has made herself ready. Fine linen, bright and clean, was given her to wear. (Fine linen stands for the righteous acts of the saints.)"

We might have expected the fine linen to stand for the righteousness of Christ or the faith of the saints. But we're told it stands instead for the righteous *acts* or *works* of the saints.

When it comes to works, many of us Protestants have thrown out the baby with the bathwater. We've gotten the erroneous idea that to God "works" is a dirty word. True, he says no works can earn salvation (Isaiah 64:6) and condemns doing works to impress others (Matthew 6:1-18). But our Lord enthusiastically commends works done for the right reasons.

Often Ephesians 2:8-9 is quoted and verse 10 is left off. Immediately after saying our salvation is "not by works," Paul adds: "For we are God's workmanship, created in Christ Jesus to do good works, which God prepared in advance for us to do."

Rather than condemning good works, this passage elevates them. Why did God create us? *To do good works.* He's prepared a lifetime of good works for us to do. Are we doing them? He's watching, he's keeping track (Revelation 2–3), and he will reward us accordingly.

Scripture ties God's reward-giving to his very character: "God is not unjust; he will not forget your work and the love you have shown him as you have helped his people and continue to help them" (Hebrews 6:10).

Good works are essential to the Christian life (James 2:17-26; 3:13). Our faith is demonstrated by our actions; a life of service to God and others is the natural outflow of faith.

Christ will say to some believers, "Well done, good and faithful servant" (Matthew 25:21). Notice that he won't say "Well *said*" or "Well *believed*," but "Well *done*."

Peter said, "If you *do* these things, you will never fall, and you will receive a rich welcome into the eternal kingdom of our Lord and Savior Jesus Christ" (2 Peter 1:10-11). What a powerful encouragement to the Christian who has sacrificed in this life to prepare for the next. In heaven there awaits him a great welcoming committee. But this is not automatic—the conditional "if…then" suggests that if we don't do what Peter prescribes, we won't receive as rich a welcome when we enter heaven.

Where we spend eternity, whether heaven or hell, will be determined by our faith (itself a gift of God). Our further station in either place will be determined by our works. John Bunyan said, "Consider, to provoke you to good works, that you shall have from God, when you come to glory, a reward for everything you do for him on earth."

Our rewards in heaven will link us eternally to our service for Christ while on earth—even when that service seemed as unrewarding as gathering stones from dark riverbeds.

The Bible teaches two eternal judgments of two types of people—unbelievers and believers. At the judgment of faith before God's "great white throne," all true believers will pass while all unbelievers will fail, since their names are "not found written in the book of life" (Revelation 20:11-15).

But faith isn't the only thing to be judged. Scripture repeatedly states we'll be judged for our works. Jesus says to Christians, "I am he who searches hearts and minds, and I will repay each of you according to your deeds" (Revelation 2:23).

"God will bring every deed into judgment, including every hidden thing, whether it is good or evil" (Ecclesiastes 12:14). "For we will all stand before God's judgment seat.… So then, each of us will give an account of himself to God" (Romans 14:10,12).

This doctrine is as basic and ancient as the church itself. The statement that "Christ will come again to judge the living and the dead" found its way into the Apostles Creed (A.D. 250), the Nicene Creed (A.D. 325), and the Athanasian Creed (A.D. 400).

For unbelievers, this judgment of works comes at the Great White Throne judgment. Though believers will not be subject to that judgment, we will face a judgment of works at what is called the "judgment seat of Christ," where "each one may receive what is due him for the things done while in the body, whether good or bad" (2 Corinthians 5:10).

Those words "whether good or bad" are perhaps the most disturbing ones for believers in the New Testament. I've found that any honest attempts to deal with this passage are met with tremendous resistance. Equally disturbing is Paul's statement to Christians in Colossians 3:25 that "anyone who does wrong will be repaid for his wrong, and there is no favoritism."

Scripture teaches with unmistakable clarity that all believers in Christ will give an account of their lives to their Lord. The result of this judgment will be the gain or loss of eternal rewards. Each believer will "receive what is due him" (2 Corinthians 5:10). He may "receive his reward" or he may "suffer loss" (1 Corinthians 3:14-15).

Obviously, God's Word treats this judgment with great sobriety. It never portrays it as a meaningless formality, a going-through-the-motions before we get on to the real business of heavenly bliss. Rather, the Christian's judgment is a monumental event in which things of eternal significance are brought to light and things of eternal consequence are put into effect.

Our "works" are simply what we've done with our resources—our time, our energy, our talents, our money, our possessions. The fire of God's holiness will reveal the quality and the eternal significance of what we've done with our God-given assets. If our works are made of the right stuff (gold, silver, costly stones), they'll withstand and be purified by the fire. But if their essence is no more than wood or hay or straw, then no matter how nice they've been made to look in the display case of this world, they won't withstand the incendiary gaze of God's Son in the next.

"Let us throw off everything that hinders and the sin that so easily entangles, and let us run with perseverance the race marked out for us" (Hebrews 12:1). Sin entangles us, puts us out of the competition, and results in our losing both the race and the prize.

True, God is for us, not against us (Romans 8:31). He wants to commend us at the judgment seat of Christ. He doesn't want the works of our lifetime to go up in smoke.

He *wants* us to have eternal rewards and has provided every possible resource—from his Holy Spirit within to the Word of God to the Body of Christ—to help us do so. God has given us "everything we need" to live the godly life that results in eternal rewards (2 Peter 1:3).

That's why, when we really understand it, this subject should be encouraging to us. "It is my happiness," John Calvin wrote, "that I have served him who never fails to reward his servants to the full extent of his promise."

Eighteen

Salvation, Rewards, and Forgiveness

I know what you're thinking: If Christ has paid the price for our sin, and if we've confessed our sins and been forgiven, how can we be held accountable for what we've done?

It's critical to understand that the judgment of believers by Christ is a judgment of our works, not our sins. In 1 Corinthians 3:13-14, Paul says of each believer, "His *work* will be shown for what it is," and God's judgment fire "will test the quality of each man's *work.*"

Our sins are totally forgiven when we come to Christ, and we stand justified in him. There's no condemnation for the Christian (Romans 8:1). Nevertheless, our laying up of precious stones on the foundation of Christ can apparently be replaced or prevented by sins we've committed as well as by righteous acts we've failed to do. Therefore a believer's sins contribute directly to his being able to "suffer loss" (1 Corinthians 3:15).

Through this loss of reward the believer is considered to be receiving his "due" for his bad works (2 Corinthians 5:10). This is not a punishment for sins, but the withholding of rewards for works not done that should have been.

Let's be sure this is perfectly clear: Salvation and rewards are different.

Salvation is about *God's work for us.* It's a free gift, to which we can contribute absolutely nothing (Ephesians 2:8-9; Titus 3:5).

Rewards are about *our work for God.*

Salvation is dependent on God's faithfulness to his promises and on his mercy.

Rewards are conditional, dependent on our faithfulness (2 Timothy 2:12; Revelation 2:26-28; 3:21).

Belief determines our eternal destination…where we'll be.

Behavior determines our eternal rewards…what we'll have.

Works do *not* affect our redemption. Works *do* affect our reward. Just as there are eternal consequences to our faith, so there are eternal consequences to our works.

Because we speak of rewards so rarely, when we do speak of them, it's easy to confuse God's work and man's. We may, for example, mistakenly believe that heaven is a person's reward for doing good things. This is absolutely *not* the case. Eternal life is entirely "the gift of God" (Romans 6:23). In going to heaven we don't get what we deserve. What we all deserve is hell. Heaven is a gift, not a reward. Even our faith itself is God's gift (Ephesians 2:8).

In regard to salvation, our work for God is no substitute for God's work for us. In regard to rewards, God's work for us is no substitute for our work for God. Of course, this doesn't mean we work in our own strength to earn rewards. Ultimately even our reward-earning works are empowered by the Holy Spirit (Colossians 1:29).

Eternal rewards are guaranteed; *temporal* rewards are not.

Someday, as a servant of God, I will stand before my Master and my works will be evaluated. He will reward me accordingly. But in the meantime Scripture does not guarantee I will always receive rewards on earth.

I may have to suffer for righteousness' sake (1 Peter 3:14-17). "In fact, everyone who wants to live a godly life in Christ Jesus will be persecuted" (2 Timothy 3:12).

For the moment, the cynical expression sometimes proves true: "No good deed goes unpunished." But *only* for the moment. When he suffered, Jesus "made no threats. Instead, he entrusted himself to him who judges justly" (1 Peter 2:23). In the end, our righteous God promises to make all things right.

But when it comes to my bad works and my failure to do good works, it gets tricky. Where does *forgiveness* fit in all this?

In the arena of salvation, the question of forgiveness for our sins has every bearing on our eternal destination. If we've trusted Christ for his forgiveness and provision of life, we will *not* pay the eternal price of our sins. Jesus went to hell for us on the cross. He has fully forgiven our sins, and we are completely secure in his love (Psalm 103:8-18; Romans 8:31-39).

But in the arena of rewards, forgiveness of sins isn't the issue. We are forgiven—if we weren't, we wouldn't go to heaven and be standing before the judgment seat of Christ in the first place. But the Bible teaches that there can be certain consequences of our actions even when we're completely forgiven.

Suppose I got drunk and drove my car seventy miles per hour down a back street, hitting and killing a six-year-old girl. If I sincerely repented, would God forgive me? Of course. Would the fact that he forgave me bring the girl back to life? Would it keep me from being prosecuted? Of course not.

Forgiveness means God eliminates eternal condemnation. But it does not mean our actions in this life have no consequences on earth—a forgiven person can still get AIDS or the death penalty. Neither does it mean they have no consequences in eternity—a forgiven person can still lose his reward and forfeit a position of leadership in the kingdom (Revelation 3:11).

Once lost or squandered, opportunity doesn't reappear. We shouldn't let past failure plague us (Philippians 3:13-14). But we should take steps to avoid missing future opportunities.

While in Greece, my missionary friend Dan Vorm and I spent a day in ancient Corinth. For an hour we sat on the same judgment seat Paul stood before in Acts 18, the same one he used to help the Corinthian Christians visualize Christ's future judgment of the believer. Together we read Scriptures that speak of that day when we'll stand before the Lord's judgment seat and give an account for what we have done. We discussed the implications and prayed that, when that day comes, he will find us faithful and say to us, "Well done."

Dan and I prayed knowing that our hourly and daily choices will determine what transpires on the day of judgment. Yes, God is fully sovereign and it is only by his grace that we can make right choices. Yet he calls upon us to make those choices and says he will hold us accountable for them.

That hour on the Bema seat at Corinth was one of the most sobering hours of my life. By God's grace, I want to be ready for the real judgment seat of Christ. As many times as I've failed him,

I want to experience the joy of hearing him look over my life as a whole and say, "Well done."

If you wonder if there's anything you've done that God could possibly reward, be encouraged by 1 Corinthians 4:5 which talks of the judgment when "*each* will receive his praise from God." He will find something to reward you for. The question is, will you seek to do more rewardable works for him now, while you still can?

Anticipating this future joy should fuel our present ministry efforts. Let's live in light of the words of John Bunyan, the pastor who wrote *Pilgrim's Progress* in prison:

> Whatever good thing you do for him, if done according to the Word, is laid up for you as treasure in chests and coffers, to be brought out to be rewarded before both men and angels, to your eternal comfort.

Nineteen

Treasures and Crowns

Mark was walking home from school one day when the boy ahead of him tripped and dropped his books, two sweaters, a baseball glove, and other odds and ends. Mark knelt down and helped the boy pick up the scattered items. Since they were going the same way, he helped carry some of the stuff.

As they walked Mark discovered the boy's name was Bill, that he loved baseball and history, that he was having trouble with his other subjects, and that his girlfriend had just broken up with him.

They arrived at Bill's house and spent the afternoon in small talk and some laughs before Mark went home. They continued to see each other around school, had lunch together a few times, then both graduated from junior high. They ended up in the same high school where they had brief contacts over the years.

Just three weeks before graduation, Bill asked Mark if they could talk.

Bill reminded him of the day five years ago when they first met. "Did you ever wonder why I was carrying so many things home that day?" he asked. "I cleaned out my locker because I didn't want to leave a mess for anyone else. I'd stored away some of my mom's sleeping pills, and I was going home to commit suicide. But after we spent time together talking and laughing, it turned things around for me. You see, Mark, when you picked up those books that day, you did a lot more; you saved my life."

Mark found this out five years later. But in most cases we won't hear the rest of the story until we get to heaven.

How many times have we done small acts of kindness on earth without realizing the effects? How many times have we shared Christ with someone we thought didn't take it to heart, but years later they came to the Lord partly because of the seeds we planted? How many times have we spoken up for unborn children and seen no result, but without our knowledge someone chose not to have an abortion, and a life was saved? How many dishes have been washed and diapers changed and crying children sung to in the middle of the night, when we couldn't see the impact of the love we showed? How many times have we prayed and not seen an answer, when God was doing something great we won't ever know about until heaven?

God is watching. He's keeping track. In heaven he'll reward us for our acts of faithfulness to him, right down to every cup of cold water we've given to the needy in his name (Mark 9:41).

I've reminded myself of this when doing pro-life work, which often doesn't have obvious or immediate fruit. Those who spend their lives reaching out to Muslims and in other "low fruit" ministries should remember God says, "It is required in stewards, that a man be found *faithful*," not *successful* (1 Corinthians 4:2, KJV). Of course, we want to be successful, but we can't control the results. Those we must leave to God, reminding ourselves that one day we'll learn of eternal results we never saw on earth. (Just as some of us may learn in heaven that our earthly ministries weren't as successful as everyone thought.)

While heaven will be wonderful for all its inhabitants, Scripture makes it clear that not every believer's position and experience in heaven will be the same. Heaven's rewards—its possessions and positions—will vary from person to person.

Not all of us will hear the master say, "Well done, good and faithful servant" (Matthew 25:23). Not all will have treasure in heaven (Matthew 6:19-21). Not all will have the same positions of authority in heaven (Luke 19:17-26). We'll have differing levels of reward (1 Corinthians 3:12-15). Scripture suggests some Christians will be ashamed at Christ's coming (1 John 2:28). I don't think this shame will continue in heaven, but there's no indication that rewards lost due to disobedience on earth will ever be restored.

Just as heaven will be wonderful for all and even better for some, hell will be terrible for all and even worse for some. Punishment will vary according to the nature and number of the sins committed (Revelation 20:12-13). Jesus warned that people in certain towns where he ministered would have a worse fate on the day of judgment than that of other cities (Matthew 11:20-24).

The notion of differences in heaven strikes many as unfair. We've gotten the false impression that heaven must be identical for all of us.

If everyone will be happy in heaven, what's the nature of the differences? The best explanation is differing capacity. Two jars can both be full, but the bigger jar contains more. Likewise, all of us will be full of joy in heaven, but some may have more joy because their capacity for joy will be larger, having been stretched through their trust in God and obedience to him in this life.

John Bunyan said, "He who is most in the bosom of God, and who so acts for him here, he is the man who will be best able to enjoy most of God in the kingdom of heaven."

No matter how we attempt to explain it, no matter how incompatible it seems with what we've heard, it's a fact of Scripture that there will be differing rewards and differing positions in heaven. This adds up to different experiences in heaven that are now being forged in the crucible of *this* life.

What will those rewards consist of? Crowns are a common symbol of rulership. Five crowns are specifically mentioned as heavenly rewards:

1. *The Crown of Life*—for faithfulness to Christ in persecution or martyrdom (James 1:12; Revelation 2:10).

2. *The Incorruptible Crown*—for determination, discipline, and victory in the Christian life (1 Corinthians 9:24-25).

3. *The Crown of Glory*—for faithfully representing Christ in a position of spiritual leadership (1 Peter 5:1-4).

4. *The Crown of Righteousness*—for purifying and readying ourselves to meet Christ at his return (2 Timothy 4:6-8).

5. *The Crown of Rejoicing*—for pouring ourselves into others in evangelism and discipleship (1 Thessalonians 2:19; Philippians 4:1). This crown may relate to Daniel 12:3, which says, "Those who lead many to righteousness" will shine "like the stars for ever and ever."

There may be innumerable crowns and types of crowns as

well as many rewards unrelated to crowns. All are graciously given by the Lord Jesus and earned through the faithful efforts of the believer. They are lasting reminders of our work on earth and Christ's faithfulness in empowering us to do that work.

Our rewards are given not merely for our recognition, but for Christ's. We see this in Revelation 4:10-11, where the twenty-four elders "fall down before him who sits on the throne" and lay their crowns before his feet while they worship and praise him.

Though God's glory is the highest and ultimate reason for any course of action, Scripture sees no contradiction between God's eternal glory and our eternal good. On the contrary, glorifying God will always result in our greatest eternal good. Likewise, pursuing our eternal good—as he commands us to—will always glorify God.

"Hold on to what you have, so that no one will take your crown" (Revelation 3:11). We can be disqualified from earning our crowns (1 Corinthians 9:27), and we can lose them (1 Corinthians 3:15) or have them taken from us (Matthew 25:28-29). When we seek our rewards from men, we forfeit rewards from God (Matthew 6:5-6).

John warns, "Watch out that you do not lose what you have worked for, but that you may be rewarded fully" (2 John 8). Not only can we fail to receive rewards, through acts of unfaithfulness we can also forfeit rewards already in our account.

I recently read a Christian author who categorically states that people won't own anything in heaven.

But what about the different dwelling places believers will have in heaven (Luke 16:4,9)? What about the treasures Christ commanded us to store up for ourselves in heaven (Matthew 6:20)? What about the different crowns and rewards God will hand out according to our works (2 Corinthians 5:10)? What about the fact that we have an inheritance that will be given us in heaven (Colossians 3:24)? Doesn't the word *inheritance* imply something tangible that will belong to us?

Will your crown be as much mine as yours? Of course not. What about God's promise to give to overcomers a white stone with our new name written on it, a name no one else will know (Revelation 2:17)? Will you and I have equal possession of those stones or names? No. The one God gives you will be yours, not mine. The one he gives me—if I'm an overcomer—will be mine, not yours. Is this ownership wrong or selfish? Of course not. Ownership is never wrong when it's God distributing to us possessions he wants us to own!

Heaven is not a socialist utopia in which private ownership is evil. Materialism, greed, envy, and selfishness are sins; ownership is not.

Our different personalities, rewards, positions, and names in heaven speak not only of our individuality but of how God, who loves us all, finds unique reasons to love us. I love my wife and daughters, and I love different things about each.

We are like unique instruments, played by an orchestra of individual musicians performing as one. We will play together in perfect unity, but each of us will play our own part in bringing glory to God. We all will bring something different, something singular and vital, to the concert of praise. Perhaps each of us will uniquely draw attention to one of his attributes. And God will take delight in each uniqueness, for he is not a God of sameness but of diversity.

Believers will reign with Christ (Revelation 20:6). "Reigning" implies delegating responsibilities to those under our leadership. One parable tells us certain believers will be put "in charge of many things" (Matthew 25:21,23). Christ spoke of granting some of his followers leadership over specific numbers of cities in proportion to their faithful service on earth (Luke 19:12-19).

Real cities? Sure, why not? The New Jerusalem is heaven's capital city, but that doesn't mean it's the only city. God can spread cities across the new earth, the new galaxy, and the new universe.

We'll even have angels under our command (1 Corinthians 6:2-3). Where will we send them? On what missions? What responsibilities will we delegate to angels? We don't know yet. But don't you look forward to finding out?

Conditions for reigning are clearly stated in several passages, with an emphasis on endurance and perseverance: "If we endure, we will also reign with him" (2 Timothy 2:12). "To him who overcomes," Christ promises, "I will give the right to sit with me on my throne" (Revelation 3:21).

Christ also promises, "To him who overcomes and does my will to the end, I will give authority over the nations...just as I have received authority from my Father. I will also give him the morning star" (Revelation 2:26-28).

The "morning star" was the name for the planet Venus. Perhaps this suggests God's servants will reign not only over this world but others.

God alone judges the motives of the heart (1 Corinthians 4:5). Accordingly, he will reward small and hidden acts of faithfulness (Mark 9:41). He will also disregard many public acts of notoriety that might impress us (Matthew 6:1-18).

Think about this not only when you look in the mirror, but when you look at your family, neighbors, acquaintances, the man at the office, the girl behind the counter, the taxi driver, the Down Syndrome child, and the handicapped old woman who spends her days praying for missionaries. (Take a very close look, since you and I may be serving under her in heaven.)

In *The Weight of Glory* C. S. Lewis said,

> It is a serious thing to remember that the dullest and most uninteresting person you can talk to may one day be a creature which, if you saw it now, you would be strongly tempted to worship, or else a horror and a corruption such as you now meet, if at all, only in a nightmare. All day long we are, in some degree, helping each other to one or other of these destinations. It is in the light of these overwhelming possibilities, it is with the awe and the circumspection proper to them, that we should conduct all our dealings with one another, all friendships, all loves, all play, all politics. There are no ordinary people. You have never talked to a mere mortal. Nations, cultures, arts, civilizations—these are mortal, and their life is to ours as the life of a gnat. But it is immortals whom we joke with, work with, marry, snub, and exploit—immortal horrors or everlasting splendors.

Twenty

God's Way of Rewarding

Two men owned farms side by side. One was a bitter atheist, the other a devout Christian. Constantly annoyed at the Christian for his trust in God, the atheist said to him one winter, "Let's plant our crops as usual this spring, each the same number of acres. You pray to your God and I'll curse him. Then come October, let's just see who has the bigger crop."

When October came, the atheist was delighted because his crop was larger. "See, you fool," he taunted. "What do you have to say for your God now?"

"My God," replied the other farmer, "doesn't settle all his accounts in October."

God's compensation for both believers and unbelievers is usually deferred. But a day is coming upon all men, when the announcement from heaven will ring out, "The time has come for judging...and for rewarding" (Revelation 11:18). This will be the "appointed time" of judgment (1 Corinthians 4:5). "At the proper time," Paul says elsewhere, "we will reap a harvest if we do not give up." So he encourages us, "Let us not become weary in doing good" (Galatians 6:9).

Just as God has his proper time for judgment and rewards, he has his proper way of doing it.

God will reward us generously. Jesus promised a return of "a hundred times" (Matthew 19:29). This is essentially a promise of infinite return, a return far out of proportion to the amount originally invested.

God will reward us fairly. "He has set a day when he will judge the world *with justice*" (Acts 17:31). "I the LORD search the heart and examine the mind, to reward a man according to his conduct, *according to what his deeds deserve*" (Jeremiah 17:10). The answer to Abraham's rhetorical question in Genesis 18:25—"Will not the Judge of all the earth do right?"—is clearly "yes."

There is built into every person, in every society and religion, a basic belief that good deserves reward, evil deserves punishment, and eventually both will get what they deserve. Scripture confirms that God gives all people an inner awareness of his moral law: "The requirements of the law are written on their hearts" (Romans 2:15).

God will judge us with total knowledge. "Nothing in all creation is hidden from God's sight. Everything is uncovered and laid bare before the eyes of him to whom we must give account" (Hebrews 4:13). "He will bring to light what is hidden in darkness" (1 Corinthians 4:5). "For God will bring every deed into judgment, including every hidden thing, whether it is good or evil" (Ecclesiastes 12:14).

Nothing will remain secret or confidential. As Nick learns in *Edge of Eternity,* "There's no such thing as a private moment."

Since God's knowledge is total, his judgment will be comprehensive and detailed. In fact, "men will have to give account on the day of judgment for every careless word they have spoken" (Matthew 12:36). (Coupled with James 3, this is a powerful motivation for learning to think and pray before we speak.)

God will judge us with complete understanding. God knows our innermost intentions and will judge us in light of them: "He will...expose the motives of men's hearts" (1 Corinthians 4:5). His Word "judges the thoughts and attitudes of the heart" (Hebrews 4:12).

God promises to grant you rewards in light of your faithfulness and good motives (1 Corinthians 4:2,5), your life of godliness (2 Peter 3:11-14), and your faithful obedience (Matthew 25:20-21).

He will not overlook anyone or anything: "The Lord will reward everyone for whatever good he does" (Ephesians 6:8). In dispensing rewards, Christ will not neglect your smallest acts of thoughtfulness (Mark 9:41).

When you extend hospitality and give a meal to those too poor or incapacitated to pay you back, Christ promises, "Although they cannot repay you, you will be repaid at the resurrection of the righteous" (Luke 14:14).

God will reward you for kindness to the undeserving. If you "love your enemies, do good to them, and lend to them without expecting to get anything back," Christ promises, "your reward will be great" (Luke 6:35).

God will reward you for wise and productive use of the resources and opportunities he has given you (Matthew 25:14-23).

If you endure difficult circumstances because you've placed your trust in God, you will be "richly rewarded" (Hebrews 10:35). If you persevere under persecution for your faith, Jesus promises, "great is your reward in heaven" (Luke 6:23).

Paul said, "Our light and momentary troubles are achieving for us an eternal glory that far outweighs them all" (2 Corinthians 4:17). Paul's troubles certainly weren't light by our standards (2 Corinthians 11:23-29). But they were the raw materials God used to forge eternal rewards in heaven.

Every trial we face, every pain we endure, God can use to multiply and enhance what awaits us in heaven. This is why after talking about how momentary troubles achieve eternal glory, Paul says, "So we fix our eyes not on what is seen [present sufferings], but on what is unseen [future rewards]. For what is seen is temporary, but what is unseen is eternal" (2 Corinthians 4:18).

God also promises to reward you for identifying with those who are suffering for Christ and for taking material loss in order to serve him:

> You sympathized with those in prison and joyfully accepted the confiscation of your property, because you knew that you yourselves had better and lasting possessions.
>
> So do not throw away your confidence; it will be richly rewarded. You need to persevere so that when you have done the will of God, you will receive what he has promised. (Hebrews 10:34-36)

God doesn't just give us permission to get excited about future rewards—he delights in our wanting them. In fact, he says anyone coming to God "must believe...that he rewards those who earnestly seek him" (Hebrews 11:6). God is by his nature a rewarder and calls upon us to seek the rewards he offers.

There persists among many Christians the belief that desire for rewards in heaven is crass, and that to pursue rewards from God is selfish and mercenary. The Bible teaches otherwise.

Paul ran his race with his eyes on heaven's prize (Philippians 3:13-14), which motivated him to run hard and long. He was unashamedly motivated by the prospect of eternal reward and acknowledged it freely and frequently (1 Corinthians 9:24-25; 2 Corinthians 4:16-18; 5:9-10; 2 Timothy 4:7-8). "Run in such a way as to get the prize," he said, and on the verge of death he spoke longingly of the crown the Judge would award him in heaven.

Paul encouraged this same motivation to good works for all believers. Slaves are told, "You will receive an inheritance from the Lord as a reward" (Colossians 3:22-25). The rich are warned not to put their hope in wealth, but "to be rich in good deeds." Why? So they can "lay up treasure for themselves as a firm foundation for the coming age" (1 Timothy 6:17-19).

We're used to the idea that Satan tempts us by offering us power, possessions, and pleasures. But we forget it's God who made our desires for these things, not as part of our sin nature, but as part of our human nature. That's why Satan tempted the sinless Christ with pleasure, power, and possessions (Matthew

4:1-11), just as he tempted Adam and Eve before they were sinners (Genesis 3:1-7).

In fact, God himself appeals to each of these desires in us. He offers us the reward of *power* in his eternal kingdom (Matthew 20:20-28; Luke 12:42-44; Luke 19:15-19), *possessions* in his eternal kingdom (Matthew 6:19-21; 19:16-22, 27-30), and *pleasures* in his eternal kingdom (Psalm 16:11). Our goal is to attain these treasures in heaven, not on earth, through humble acts of service and generosity, not selfishness and lording it over others.

In offering these things, God does not tempt us (James 1:13). It's not wrong for us to be motivated by the prospect of reward. Indeed, something is wrong if we're *not* motivated by reward. To resist wanting rewards is pseudospiritual. It goes against the grain of the way God created us and the way he tries to motivate us.

Suppose I tell one of my daughters, "If you do a full day of yard work Saturday, I'll pay you $60 and take you out to a nice dinner." Would it be wrong for her to want to earn the $60? Would it be wrong for her to look forward to going out to a nice dinner? Of course it wouldn't be wrong. I made the offer, and I *want* her to want those things.

"But God doesn't owe us anything. He has the right to expect us to work for him with no thought of reward." True, he owes us nothing. And yes, we should be willing to serve him with no thought of payoff, simply because it's our duty and we're unworthy servants (Luke 17:7-10). So, if we were the ones who came to him and said, "God, we're not going to serve you for nothing; you owe us for this," we would be dead wrong. But here's the point—our receiving reward for serving God is not *our* idea. It's *his* idea.

If my daughter did the yard work joylessly, then said, "No, Dad, I refuse the money and I don't want to go to dinner with you," how would that make me feel?

Too many of us consider incentives to be "secular" or "unspiritual." But God made us the way we are. By his own design all of us need incentives to motivate us to do our jobs and do them well.

He'll reward the child who gave to the missions offering the money she'd saved for a softball mitt. He'll reward the teenager who kept himself pure despite all the temptations. He'll reward the man who tenderly cared for his wife with Alzheimer's, the mother who raised the child with cerebral palsy, the child who rejoiced in his heart despite his handicap. He'll reward the unskilled who were faithful and the skilled who were meek and servant-hearted. He'll reward the parents who modeled Christ to their children and the children who followed him despite the bad example of their parents. He'll reward those who suffered while trusting him and those who helped the suffering.

"For the Son of Man is going to come in his Father's glory with his angels, and then he will reward each person *according to what he has done*" (Matthew 16:27).

Martin Luther said that on his calendar there were only two days: "today" and "that Day." May we invest all that we are and have today in light of that Day.

Twenty-one

Second Chances?

There's an old story of a slave who travels with his master to Baghdad. Early one morning, milling through the marketplace, the slave sees Death in human form. Death gives him a threatening look, and the slave recoils in terror, convinced Death intends to take him that day.

The slave runs to his master and says, "Help me! I've seen Death, and his threatening look tells me he intends to take my life this very day. I must escape him. Please let me leave now and flee on my camel so tonight I can reach Samarra, where Death cannot find me."

His master agrees, and the terrified servant takes off on the fifteen-hour journey to Samarra.

A few hours later, the master himself sees Death among the throngs in Baghdad. He boldly approaches Death and asks him, "Why did you give my servant a threatening look?"

"That was not a threatening look," Death replies. "That was a look of surprise. I was amazed to see your servant today in Baghdad, for I have an appointment with him tonight in Samarra."

While the imagery is pagan, the central moral of the story is biblical. "No man has power over the wind to contain it; so no one has power over the day of his death" (Ecclesiastes 8:8).

We may spend our lives running from death and denying death, but that won't stop death from coming at its appointed time.

Not talking about death won't postpone it. Talking about death won't bring it a moment sooner. But it *will* give us opportunity to be better prepared when it comes. That's why our family periodically talks about death, reminding ourselves we should be ready, and if one of us dies soon (one of these times we will), we'll see each other in heaven.

Since life's greatest certainty is death, it only makes sense to prepare for what lies beyond. Any life that leaves us unprepared for death is a foolish life. Matthew Henry said, "It ought to be the business of every day to prepare for our last day."

In *Edge of Eternity*, the King tells Nick the truth for all of us: "A moment after a man dies he knows exactly how he should have lived. But then it's too late for him to go back and live differently. After death, there is no second chance."

This isn't what Nick wanted to hear:

My mind raced through my life like a fallen leaf down powerful rapids. I thirsted for the undiscovered country that beckoned me. But I also yearned inconsolably for a second chance, an opportunity to do it all over, to make things right. But I'd squandered my opportunities. I'd missed my chance.

Nick discovered, as we must, that earth alone is the land of second chances.

God's rewards are eternal and irrevocable. The tangible results of our choices on earth will carry over into eternity.

Just as the unbeliever cannot come back to earth and live his life over again and this time trust Christ, so also there's no opportunity for the believer to go back and relive his life, this time in faithful service to Christ.

We might hope that what happens at the judgment seat will be of only temporary concern to the Judge. We might wish all our disobedience and missed opportunities will just "blow over"— that none of it will ever make any real difference. But will God consider a life of selfishness and indifference to others' needs to be as worthy of reward as a life spent in quiet faithfulness and prayer and feeding the hungry and sharing the gospel? The Bible clearly says "no."

You can't do life on earth over again. There's no retaking the course, trying to improve a D to an A. There's no rescheduling of the final exams. Ready or not, they come at the appointed time. (We just don't happen to know what it is.)

Your death will be like the final buzzer at a basketball game. No shots taken thereafter will count. If you've failed to use your money and possessions and time and talent and energies for eternity, then you've failed—period.

At your death, the autobiography you've written with the pen of faith and the ink of works will go into eternity unedited, to be seen and read "as is" by angels, the redeemed, and God himself.

"Well, I'll be in heaven, and that's all that matters." How dare we say that when so much else matters to God? Scripture speaks of loss of reward as a great and terrible loss. The fact that an unrewarded believer is still saved is only a clarification, not a consolation: "He himself will be saved, but only as one escaping through the flames" (1 Corinthians 3:15).

Missionary martyr Jim Elliot said it so well: "He is no fool who gives what he cannot keep to gain what he cannot lose."

Look again to C. S. Lewis's *The Weight of Glory:*

> If we consider the unblushing promises of rewards promised in the Gospels, it would seem that our Lord finds our desires not too strong, but too weak. We are half-hearted creatures, fooling about with drink and sex and ambition when infinite joy is offered us, like an ignorant child who wants to go on making mud pies in a slum because he cannot imagine what is meant by the offer of a holiday at the sea. We are far too easily pleased.

He who gives his time and talents and money and possessions to earn rewards from his God—the greatest of which is the resounding "well done"—is one whose deepest thirsts will be eternally quenched by the Maker and Fulfiller of Desire.

With such a prospect available to us, why would we devote our lives to the "mud pies" of this world's treasures? Why not devote them to the extraordinary joys of heaven that can be ours forever?

Are you too easily pleased?

Twenty-two

What Difference Does It Make?

When my friend Leona Bryant discovered she had only a short time to live, she told me of her radical changes in perspective. "The most striking thing that's happened," she said, "is that I find myself totally uninterested in all the conversations about material things. Things used to matter to me, but now I find my thoughts are never on possessions, but always on Christ and people. I consider it a privilege to live each day knowing I'll die soon. What a difference it makes!"

Have you, like David, asked God to help you remember what we so easily forget?

> Show me, O LORD, my life's end
> and the number of my days;
> let me know how fleeting is my life. (Psalm 39:4)

Since this life is so brief, we might conclude it is inconsequential. Our lives seem like a pebble dropped in a pond, creating tiny ripples that quickly disappear. A look at abandoned tombstones with names no one remembers is a stark reminder of our eventual anonymity in this world. What do you know about your great-grandfather? What will your great-grandchildren know about you?

Our brief stay here may seem unimportant, but that's an illusion. The Bible tells us that while men may not remember or care what our lives here have been, God remembers perfectly and cares very much—so much that the door of eternity swings on the hinges of choices made here and now.

This life is the headwaters out of which life in heaven flows. Eternity will hold for us what we've poured into it during our lives here. Your God-given resources of time and talents and money and possessions are the lever, positioned on the fulcrum of this life, that moves the mountains of eternity.

When you see today in light of the long tomorrow, even the little choices become tremendously important. Reading your Bible today, praying, going to church, sharing your faith, and giving your money to further God's kingdom are of eternal consequence, not only for other souls but for your own.

During the developing process, a photograph is immersed in different solutions. As long as the photo is in the developing fluid, it's subject to change and adjustment. But when it's placed in the "stop bath" or "fixer," the image becomes permanently fixed. Life on earth is like being in the developing fluid. Death is the fixer that forever freezes the image of our lives.

After death, you and I will never have another chance to share Christ with one who can be saved from hell, to give a cup of water to the thirsty, to serve our church, to invest money to help the helpless and reach the lost, or to open our homes and give to the poor and needy.

No wonder Scripture makes clear that the one central business of this life is to prepare for the next.

Materialism would dupe us into believing this world is the ultimate world, the destination rather than the route to the Destination. From there it's a short step to racing off to earn, collect, accumulate, take, and consume as if that's all there is to life. Then we wake up one day (if we ever wake up at all) to realize how terribly unhappy we are. Joyless, passionless, we become shriveled caricatures of what we could have been if only we'd lived in light of the person and place we were made for.

Life's great disillusionments come as we try to force our round made-for-eternity heart into the rectangular hole of this temporal earth. It just doesn't fit. *We* don't fit. No matter how far we stray from the narrow path of kingdom living, we remain children of eternity. Inside we are simply ill-suited for our present existence.

Think about the special spiritual moments you've experienced. Perhaps it was during a time of prayer, in worship at church, in a conversation with a loved one, or while you were walking on the beach or in the woods. Have you ever had a sudden sense that you were moving on the edge of eternity, briefly yet truly breaking into its circle, knowing in that moment you were exactly where you belonged, taking part in what the universe must be about?

That was a glimpse of eternity. It was the awakening of a desire lying deep within, where God has set eternity in your heart.

In *Mere Christianity*, C. S. Lewis cast light on this eternal desire:

> Creatures are not born with desires unless satisfaction for those desires exists. A baby feels hunger: well, there is such a thing as food. A duckling wants to swim: well, there is such a thing as water. Men feel sexual desire: well, there is such a thing as sex. If I find in myself a desire which no experience in this world can satisfy, the most probable explanation is that I was made for another world. If none of my earthly pleasures satisfy it, that does not prove that the universe is a fraud. Probably earthly pleasures were never meant to satisfy it, but only to arouse it, to suggest the real thing.

God is eternal. His Place is eternal. His Word is eternal. His people are eternal. Center your life around God, his place, his Word, his people, and those eternal souls who desperately long for his person and his place. Do this, and no matter what you do for a living, your days here will make a profound difference. Any honest activity—whether building a shed, driving a bus, pruning trees, changing diapers, or caring for a patient—can be an investment in God's kingdom.

Your life on earth is a dot. From that dot extends a line that goes on for all eternity. Right now you're living *in* the dot. But what are you living *for*? Are you living for the dot or for the line? Are you living for earth or for heaven? Are you living for the short today or the long tomorrow?

Twenty-three

Cultivating Your Sense
of the Eternal

How many sermons about heaven or hell have you heard lately? How many books or articles have you read about it? How many discussions about them in the last few months?

In the absence of a strong theology of heaven and eternal rewards, the western church has been permeated by "prosperity theology," the gospel of health and wealth. We've been seduced to look only to short-term rewards of material gain, physical health and safety, and human approval.

What about you? Are you following the example of the saints by longing for heaven (Hebrews 11:13-16; 2 Corinthians 5:2)? Are you cultivating a passion for God's place?

Is heaven and all it represents a central object of your attention? Have you "set your heart on things above, where Christ is seated at the right hand of God" (Colossians 3:1)? Is your heart's attention there, rather than on "earthly things" (verse 2)?

Perhaps you're afraid of becoming "so heavenly minded you're of no earthly good." There's another one of Satan's myths. On the contrary, most of us are so earthly-minded we are of no heavenly or earthly good. As C. S. Lewis said, "It is since Christians have largely ceased to think of the other world that they have become so ineffective in this one."

Writing in 1649 Richard Baxter said this in his book *The Saints' Everlasting Rest:*

> If there be so certain and glorious a rest for the saints, why is there no more industrious seeking after it? One would think, if a man did but once hear of such unspeakable glory to be obtained, and believed what he heard to be true, he should be transported with the vehemency of his desire after it, and should almost forget to eat and drink, and should care for nothing else, and speak of and inquire after nothing else, but how to get this treasure. And yet people who hear of it daily, and profess to believe it as a fundamental article of their faith, do as little mind it, or labor for it, as if they had never heard of any such thing, or did not believe one word they hear.

How much do you think about heaven? Perhaps you'll want to pick out some favorite Scriptures cited in this book and post them on the mirror, the dashboard, or refrigerator. Put them where you put pictures of your loved ones. Think about them.

Remind yourself of heaven. Sit down with your children and your grandchildren, your parents and brothers and sisters and friends and talk to them about heaven.

What could be more encouraging and exciting than to anticipate your ultimate destination, to which all others pale in comparison?

Perhaps the greatest test of eternal perspective—and opportunity to develop eternal perspective—relates to how we handle our money and possessions. Let me share some insights developed in my book *Money, Possessions and Eternity*.

Thomas à Kempis said, "Let temporal things serve your use, but the eternal be the object of your desire." John Wesley said, "I judge all things only by the price they shall gain in eternity."

Jesus told us not to store up treasures for ourselves on earth, but in heaven (Matthew 6:19-21). God favors us storing up treasures for ourselves. He just wants us to stop storing them up in the wrong place and start storing them up in the right place.

"We brought nothing into the world, and we can take nothing out of it" (1 Timothy 6:7) The old phrase "You can't take it with you" is explicitly biblical.

"You'll never see a hearse pulling a U-haul." Why? Because you can't take it with you.

John D. Rockefeller was one of the wealthiest men who ever lived. After he died his accountant was asked, "How much money did John D. leave?" His reply was classic: "He left…all of it." Again, you can't take it with you.

But in Matthew 6 Jesus adds a corollary: "Yes, you can't take it with you…but you *can* send it on ahead."

Imagine you're alive at the very end of the Civil War. You're living in the South, but your home is really in the North. While in the South you've accumulated a good deal of Confederate currency. Suppose you know for a fact the North is going to win the war and that the end could come at any time. What will you do with your Confederate money?

If you're smart, there's only one answer. You'll cash in your Confederate currency for U.S. currency—the only money that will have value once the war is over. You'll keep only enough Confederate currency to meet your basic needs for that short period until the war's over and the money will be worthless.

As believers, we've been given inside knowledge of a coming upheaval in the worldwide social and economic situation. The currency of this world will be worthless at our death or Christ's return, both of which are imminent.

This knowledge should radically affect our investment strategy. For us to accumulate vast earthly treasures in the face of the inevitable future is equivalent to stockpiling Confederate money despite our awareness of its eventual worthlessness. It's not only wrong—it's just plain stupid.

Let's use our Confederate money to purchase the currency of heaven—good works done out of love for God and others, which will last for all eternity.

A. W. Tozer wrote, "Any temporal possession can be turned into everlasting wealth. Whatever is given to Christ is immediately touched with immortality."

Jesus said, "Where your treasure is, there your heart will be also" (Matthew 6:21).

Want a heart for General Motors? Buy stock in it. Want a heart for your house or car or boat? Invest your time and money in them.

Want a heart for God? Put your treasures where God is at work. Want a heart for missions? Put your treasures in missions. Want a heart for your church's ministry? Invest your money in your church's ministry. Buy up shares in the kingdom of God. Wherever you put your treasures, your heart is sure to follow.

So you want a heart for heaven? Then put as many of your treasures there as you possibly can. Give generously, then watch how quickly and dramatically you gain vested interests in heaven.

Martin Luther said, "I have held many things in my hands and I have lost them all. But whatever I have placed in God's hands, that I still possess."

Let me ask a final question. Since Christ came to free us from bondage to the fear of death (Hebrews 2:15), and since death is the necessary doorway to take us to heaven, why is it that so many Christians today are so afraid to die?

The answer is simple—we've made this world our home. We've laid up our treasures on earth. Consequently, since every day brings us closer to our death, every day takes us further from our treasures. We end up backing into eternity, not wanting to let go of all those treasures we've accumulated.

Christ calls us to turn it around. He says to store up our treasures in heaven, not earth. That way, every day that brings us closer to our death brings us closer to our treasures. Instead of backing away from our treasures, we can spend our lives moving toward our treasures.

He who spends his life moving away from his treasures has reason to despair. He who spends his life moving toward his treasures has reason to rejoice.

Are you moving toward your treasures or away from them?

Twenty-four

More Alive
Than Ever Before

The Bible begins with God casting men out of a garden and ends with God welcoming them into a garden city. The serpent who brings sin and suffering at the beginning is thrown into the lake of fire at the end. Man's tears in Genesis 3 are wiped away by God in Revelation 21. Paradise Lost becomes Paradise Regained. More than that—Paradise Magnified.

The unfolding drama of redemption is the greatest story ever told. Jesus is the hero, who suffers terribly but is ultimately victorious. We, too, are part of the story. We are those who scorned then killed him. But incredibly, in the greatest plot twist of all time, he chooses us as his bride. Now he prepares for us a home and a wedding banquet, and he promises to come back to get us, rescuing us from a hostile world and making all things right.

This is a tragic yet triumphant story of suffering and grace and hope, so heartbreaking and joyful that all other good stories are nothing but its shadows. And it is a story that is absolutely true.

If we grasp this great story—or let it grasp us—we will truly long to live now in light of eternity.

Living in light of eternity means being prepared for the day of your death. "Man is destined to die once, and after that to face judgment" (Hebrews 9:27).

Have you ever thought about the fact that at least one family member won't be at your funeral?

You.

In the New Testament, the Greek word for *sleep* is used fourteen times in reference to death (e.g. John 11:11; Acts 7:60; 1 Thessalonians 4:13).

The term *falling asleep* is simply a description of the outer appearance of the body's inactivity and the spirit's relocation where there's rest and renewal in heaven. It isn't intended to imply unconsciousness or soul-sleep. Scripture clearly shows there's an ongoing and heightened awareness at the point of death. Being absent from the body means being immediately at home with the Lord (2 Corinthians 5:8). Death means "to depart and be with Christ" (Philippians 1:23). Jesus said to the thief on the cross, *"Today* you will be with me in paradise" (Luke 23:43). The story of the rich man and Lazarus shows immediate consciousness at death, both in heaven and hell (Luke 16:19-31).

Peter uses the word "departure," or "exodus," in reference to his own approaching death (2 Peter 1:15). Death for the Christian is God's deliverance from a place of bondage and suffering to a place of freedom and relief.

In 2 Timothy 4:6-8, Paul refers to his death with the Greek word *analousis*, meaning "to loosen." Consider some of its common usages in that culture:

- An ox being loosed from its yoke when it was finished pulling a cart.
- Pulling up tent stakes, in preparation for a journey.
- Untying a ship from dock, to let it sail away.
- Unchaining a prisoner, freeing him from confinement and suffering.
- Solving a problem—when a difficult matter was finally resolved it was said to have been "loosened."

Each of these is a graphic picture of death for the Christian.

On the one hand, the Bible calls death "the last enemy" (1 Corinthians 15:26). On the other hand, for the person whose faith and actions have prepared him for it, death is a deliverer, casting off the burdens of a hostile world and ushering him into the world for which he was made.

No matter what difficulty surrounds it, God is intimately involved and interested in the Christian's departure from this world: "Precious in the sight of the LORD is the death of his saints" (Psalm 116:15).

What we call death is a transition from a dying body in a dying world to a world of light and life. No wonder Paul says, "To die is gain" and to go to be with Christ is "better by far" (Philippians 1:21-23).

There's evidence that at death the believer will be ushered into heaven by angels (Luke 16:22). Different angels are assigned to different people (Matthew 18:10), so perhaps, as I portray in my novels, our escorts into heaven will be the angels who have served us while we were on earth (Hebrews 1:14).

I've always appreciated this depiction of death, often attributed to nineteenth-century American clergyman Henry Van Dyke:

> I'm standing on the seashore. A ship at my side spreads her white sails to the morning breeze and starts for the blue ocean. She's an object of beauty and strength and I stand and watch her until, at length, she hangs like a speck of white cloud just where the sea and the sky come down to mingle with each other. And then I hear someone at my side saying, "There, she's gone."
>
> Gone where? Gone from my sight, that is all. She is just as large in mast and hull and spar as she was when she left my side. And just as able to bear her load of living freight to the place of destination. Her diminished size is in *me*, not in her.
>
> And just at the moment when someone at my side says, "There, she is gone" there are other eyes watching her coming, and there are other voices ready to take up the glad shout, "Here she comes!"

And that, *for the Christian*, is dying.

What will happen as we set foot on heaven's shores, greeted by our loved ones? I envision it as C. S. Lewis did in the *Last Battle:* "The further up and the further in you go, the bigger everything gets. The inside is larger than the outside."

The moment we die the meager flame of this life will appear, to those we leave behind, to be snuffed out. But at that same moment on the other side, it will rage to sudden and eternal intensity—an intensity that will never dim, only grow.

On his deathbed D. L. Moody said, "Soon you will read in the newspaper that I am dead. Don't believe it for a moment. I will be more alive than ever before."

Still Being Written

Alfred Nobel was a Swedish chemist who made his fortune inventing dynamite and other powerful explosives, which were bought by governments to produce weapons. When Nobel's brother died, one newspaper accidentally printed Alfred's obituary instead. When Alfred read it, he saw himself described as a man who became rich from enabling people to kill each other in unprecedented quantities. Shaken from this assessment of his life, Nobel resolved to use his fortune to reward accomplishments that benefited humanity. One of the many rewards he funded was the Nobel Peace Prize.

Nobel had a rare opportunity—to look at the assessment of his life at its end, but to still be alive and have opportunity to change that assessment.

Let's put ourselves in Nobel's place. Let's read our own obituary—not as written by uninformed or biased men, but as an onlooking angel might write it. Consider the story of our lives written from heaven's viewpoint, fact-checked for accuracy by the Audience of One himself. Sobering? Now let's use the rest of our lives to edit that obituary into what we really want it to say.

As long as we live on earth, we're still in the land of second chances. As long as we're here, we're each still writing our life's story. No one knows how the final chapter will end until it's ended.

Earth is pregnant with both heaven and hell. Our choices cast a vote for one or the other. At our deaths, the appraisal can and will finally be made. What have we done with our lives? Have we invested them in eternity? Have we carved into the minds of our families and our church and our community a burning image of the Lord Jesus Christ? Or have we poured our lives down the rat holes of prideful ambition, irresponsibility, godlessness, materialism, or empty religion?

2 Peter 3 tells us this world and everything in it is going to burn. There's a coming holocaust of things. Revelation 18 speaks of the doomed economic world system of materialism, called "Babylon the Great." If that's what you're investing your life in, then go ahead and be depressed. You've got a lot to be depressed about!

Our denial of this obvious reality is striking. Yesterday I walked by a store displaying one line of silverware called "Eternal Gold" and another "Eternal Silver." (They weren't referring to 1 Corinthians 3:12-14.) Last night I saw a magazine advertisement in which a woman stared at a diamond and asked, "What else will be mine for the next thousand years?"

When I was a pastor, a couple came to my office and told me they wanted to be able to give more money to the church and to missions. "But we've always had this dream for a beautiful home in the country," they added, "and we can't seem to shake it. Is that wrong?"

No, it isn't. In fact, the dream of a perfect home is from God.

It's just that such a dream cannot and will not be fulfilled in this life. Our dream house is coming; we don't have to build it here. In fact, we can't. Any dream house we try building here will eventually be ravaged by time, floods, earthquakes, tornadoes, carpenter ants, or freeway bypasses—you name it.

Who would want to divert kingdom funds to a dream house on earth if he understood it's going to burn to the ground, with no insurance company left to cover the loss? Instead, why wouldn't he use his resources to send construction materials ahead to the Carpenter building his dream house in heaven?

I recommend taking a family field trip to a dump or a junkyard. Show your children all the piles of "treasures" that were once Christmas and birthday presents. Point out things costing hundreds of dollars, things that children quarreled about, friendships were lost over, honesty was sacrificed for, and marriages broke up over. Show them the remnants of battered dolls, rusted robots, and crashed cars. Let them look at the expensive furniture and electronic gadgets that now lie ravaged and useless. Point out to them that nearly everything *your* family owns will one day end up in a junkyard like this.

Then read, or ask them to read, 2 Peter 3:10-14, which says when Christ returns the whole world "will be destroyed by fire" and "the earth and everything in it will be laid bare." Then ask them the ultimate question: "When all that you owned lies abandoned, broken, burned, and useless, what will you have done that will last for eternity?"

Does that sound depressing? It shouldn't. What would be depressing is if we couldn't use our present lives and resources to make a difference for eternity. But we can. What would be depressing is if our lives ended at death. But they don't. What would be depressing is if this world was our home. But it isn't.

C. S. Lewis wrote, "Our Father refreshes us on the journey with some pleasant inns, but will not encourage us to mistake them for home."

There's something important I need to add here. As long as God keeps you on earth, it's where he wants you. Don't ever believe the devil's lie that you should take your own life. Jesus says Satan's a liar and a murderer (John 8:44). He lies to justify and rationalize his attempts to kill you by your own hand. Don't listen to the liar. Listen to the truth (John 8:32; 14:6). Don't make a terrible ending to your life's story—finish your God-given course on earth. When he's done—not before—he'll take you home in his own time and way.

Until the day when the ink dries on the manuscript of your life—which could be today or next week or next year or decades from now—what must you do to write the best ending to your story?

In the time you have left on the old earth, how will you edit your own obituary as it will be read in the new earth?

Safely Home

Bertrand Russell has been called the greatest mind of the twentieth century. Anticipating his death he said, "There is darkness without, and when I die there will be darkness within. There is no splendor, no vastness anywhere; only triviality for a moment, and then nothing."

Whether or not he repented and turned to Christ before he died, Russell now knows how terribly wrong he was in thinking human beings exist only temporarily. Death is not a hole; it's a door. We don't end; we relocate.

Russell failed to recognize what children intuitively know. Heaven is not a fairy tale. It's not some baseless dream. Heaven is an objective reality that exists independently of anyone's belief or disbelief in it. Heaven is real. So real that earth, in comparison, is but the Shadowlands.

C. S. Lewis said, "There have been times when I think we do not desire heaven, but more often I find myself wondering whether, in our heart of hearts, we have ever desired anything else.... Your place in heaven will seem to be made for you and you alone, because you were made for it stitch by stitch as a glove is made for a hand."

We long for a perfect world not just because this one isn't but because we sense there really is one. Whether or not we realize it, we're homesick for heaven.

In C. S. Lewis's *The Last Battle,* when the old Narnia and the old earth are swept into the new one, the unicorn keeps urging the travelers to come "further up and further in." You can't exhaust heaven—you can only go in deeper to discover more and more and delight more and more in what you discover. On earth, when we find what we've been looking for, delight often diminishes. In heaven it's the opposite. Delight keeps increasing—no wonder, since unlike anything on earth, what's in heaven is what we were actually looking for all along.

Elisha asked God to give his servant a glimpse of the invisible realm. He prayed, "O LORD, open his eyes so he may see." Then God "opened the servant's eyes, and he looked and saw the hills full of horses and chariots of fire all around Elisha" (2 Kings 6:17).

Moses "persevered because he saw him who is invisible" (Hebrews 11:27). How can we see the invisible? (Isn't that like hearing the inaudible?) We must meditate on what Scripture says about the spiritual realm, the *real* world. We must give serious thought to heaven, never imagining it isn't real just because we can't see it. A blind man can't see the sun, but that doesn't make it any less real.

The angel who showed John the wonders of heaven anticipated a "this can't be real" response. That's why he assured the apostle, "These words are trustworthy and true" (Revelation 22:6).

By faith we take God at his Word and believe what Scripture tells us about heaven. Then we pray, "Lord, open our eyes" and envision it in our minds according to what Scripture says about it. (If you didn't do it along the way, I suggest you go back and look up the biblical references that fill this book, giving heaven the attention it deserves.)

A. W. Tozer said,

> The church is constantly being tempted to accept this world as her home…but if she is wise she will consider that she stands in the valley between the mountain peaks of eternity past and eternity to come. The past is gone forever and the present is passing as swift as the shadow on the sundial of Ahaz. Even if the earth should continue a million years not one of us could stay to enjoy it. We do well to think of the long tomorrow.

John Wesley was shown around a vast plantation by a proud landowner. They rode their horses all day and saw only a fraction of the estate. When they sat down to dinner the man said eagerly, "Well, Mr. Wesley, what do you think?" Wesley pondered the question, then replied, "I think you're going to have a hard time leaving all this."

The more we understand this world is not our home and the more we lay up our treasures in heaven, the more we will long for heaven and the more content we'll be to leave earth behind. God doesn't expect us to long for death—he *does* expect us to long for heaven.

Why waste your life trying to feel at home in a world that's not your home?

On my office wall hangs a beautiful painting by Ron DiCianni. It's entitled *Safely Home*. (Maybe you've heard the powerful Steve Green song by that name, and it's companion song "The Faithful.") The painting portrays a man on his knees. His clothing is worn and tattered. He's walked down a long strip of blood-red entry-carpet that has led him to the foot of a throne.

The man's arms dangle at his side. He appears both exhausted and relieved, overcome with emotion. His head rests on the chest of one kneeling down to him, holding him tight in a loving embrace. The one hugging him has stepped down off the throne. It's the King, the Creator of the universe, who is also, incredibly, a man. King Jesus.

A few feet to the right are open shackles lying on the palace floor. The man had been a prisoner on earth. He'd suffered terribly at the hands of those who despised him because they despised his King. In his right hand, hanging limply to the ground, is a beautiful gold crown.

The man is a martyr. He has lived out Revelation 2:10—he's been faithful unto death, and his Lord has given him the crown of life. To many, the single most important thing is the preservation of their life on earth. To this man, obeying his Lord was more important than prolonging his earthly life. He's one of those who "did not love their lives so much as to shrink from death" (Revelation 12:11).

In the background of *Safely Home* stands an angel, reverently watching, holding out in his arms a white robe. The angel is the man's guardian. In the stonework on both sides of the carpet walkway you can see the continents of earth below.

Several things strike me in this painting. One is heaven's view of earth below. Another is the look on the man's face, at long last freed from pain and persecution. But what really strikes me is the look on the face of King Jesus. He, too, is full of emotion. His face radiates compassion and approval. His nail-scarred hands, drawing the martyr to himself, are silent testimony to the extent of his love.

Ron could have named the painting *Well Done* or *Overcomer* or *No Longer a Stranger* or something else. But he named it *Safely Home*. This man who has endured great suffering is safely home at last. The evil that pursued him in the Shadowlands can no longer touch him. He's forever beyond its reach, for between evil and the man stands the Lord of the Cosmos, the one who embraces him and says, "Never again will I let you suffer."

At the moment this is going on in heaven, I imagine down on earth a wife and children, perhaps a mother and father, a church of faithful believers. They're agonizing, understandably, over what has happened to their beloved one. At the very moment they're overwhelmed with grief, the one they mourn is overcome with joy. For he is home at last. Home for the very first time.

To many people in the Shadowlands, this man has passed from life to death. In fact, it is the opposite. He has passed from death to life. And one day his believing family will join him there. Then the King will wipe away their tears too.

Regarding heaven, Scripture doesn't just say, "There will be no more tears." It says God "will wipe every tear from their eyes" (Revelation 21:4). This isn't God snapping his fingers and drying all tears from a distance. It's a very intimate picture—it means

God's hands will touch the face of each individual child, to remove every tear.

As Thomas Moore put it, "Earth has no sorrow that Heaven cannot heal." Earth is heaven's womb, and our sufferings are birth pangs.

Through his death and resurrection the Carpenter flung open the door to heaven. If you're a Christian suffering with great pains and losses, take cheer (John 16:33). The new house is almost ready for you. Moving day's coming. The dark winter is about to be magically transformed into spring. Soon you will be home.

If you're not a Christian, you need to talk to God. Don't procrastinate—time is shorter than you think. Confess and repent of your sin and ask his forgiveness (Romans 3:23; 1 John 1:9). Express your belief in Christ and ask him to make you his child (John 1:12). Accept the gift of salvation he offers (Romans 6:23). The moment you do, heaven becomes your home. Now, to sustain and guide you until you get there, find a church home that teaches the Bible and worships Christ as God and Savior. If you need help finding such a church, call us. If we don't meet on earth, I'll look forward to seeing you at home.

Our lives on earth are a training course to get us ready for heaven. It's not just that God is preparing a place for us. It's that he's preparing us for that place.

C. S. Lewis framed a great life's goal when he said,

> I must keep alive in myself the desire for my true
> country, which I shall not find till after death; I must never
> let it get snowed under or turned aside; I must make it the

main object of life to press on to that other country and to help others to do the same.

In *Edge of Eternity,* the King gives Nick the right perspective for life on earth: "Live each day as if it were your last day there. One of them will be."

The King then narrows the focus:

> "You have your orders—I send you to battle. You are a soldier, and I would not promise a soldier ease. I promise you difficulty, but with it resources and purpose and joy.
>
> "Go to where men die of thirst a stone's throw from pure water...go back as my water-bearer."

As long as we're still here in the parched wastelands of the present earth, God calls us to offer refreshment to a world full of people dying of thirst.

What should we offer them? Exactly what they thirst for—a person and a place.

Jesus is that person.

Heaven is that place.

About the Author

Randy Alcorn is the founder and director of Eternal Perspective Ministries (EPM), a nonprofit ministry devoted to promoting an eternal viewpoint and drawing attention to people in special need of advocacy and help (including the poor, the persecuted, and the unborn).

A pastor for fourteen years before founding EPM, Randy is a popular teacher and conference speaker. He's spoken in many countries and has been interviewed on over 250 radio and television programs. He's taught on the part-time faculties of Western Baptist Seminary and Multnomah Bible College. Randy lives in Gresham, Oregon, with his wife, Nanci, and daughters, Karina and Angela.

Randy produces the free quarterly issues-oriented magazine *Eternal Perspectives.* He's the author of ten previous books: *Money, Possessions and Eternity; Pro-Life Answers to Pro-Choice Arguments; Sexual Temptation; Is Rescuing Right?; Christians in the Wake of the Sexual Revolution; Does the Birth Control Pill Cause Abortions?;* and, coauthored with Nanci, *Women Under Stress.* His three novels, all bestsellers, are *Deadline, Dominion*, and *Edge of Eternity.*

Randy's life emphasis is on (1) communicating the strategic importance of using our earthly time, money, possessions, and opportunities to invest in need-meeting ministries that will count for eternity, and (2) analyzing, teaching, and applying the moral, social, and relational implications of Christian truth in the current age.

Feedback about books and inquiries regarding publications and other matters can be directed to Eternal Perspective Ministries (EPM), 2229 East Burnside #23, Gresham, OR 97030. EPM can also be reached by phone at 503-663-6481 or by e-mail via ralcorn@epm.org. For information on EPM or Randy Alcorn, and for resources on missions, pro-life issues, and matters of eternal perspective, see http://www.epm.org.

James
and the
Giant Peach

ROALD DAHL

James
and the
Giant Peach

Illustrated by Quentin Blake

ALFRED A. KNOPF
New York

THIS IS A BORZOI BOOK PUBLISHED BY ALFRED A. KNOPF

Text copyright © 1961 by Roald Dahl, renewed 1989 by Roald Dahl Nominee Limited
Illustrations copyright © 1995 by Quentin Blake
Jacket illustration copyright © 1995 by Quentin Blake
All rights reserved under International and Pan-American Copyright Conventions.
Published in the United States of America by Alfred A. Knopf, an imprint of
Random House Children's Books, a division of Random House, Inc., New York,
and simultaneously in Canada by Random House of Canada Limited, Toronto.
Distributed by Random House, Inc., New York. Originally published in different form
by Alfred A. Knopf, a division of Random House, Inc., in 1961. This illustrated edition
originally published in Great Britain by Puffin Books, The Penguin Group, in 1995.

www.randomhouse.com/kids

KNOPF, BORZOI BOOKS, and the colophon are registered trademarks of Random House, Inc.

Library of Congress Cataloging-in-Publication Data
Dahl, Roald.
James and the giant peach / Roald Dahl ; illustrated by Quentin Blake.
p. cm.
Summary: A young boy escapes from two wicked aunts and embarks on a series of adventures
with six giant insects he meets inside a giant peach.
[1. Fairy tales.] I. Blake, Quentin, ill. II. Title.
PZ8.D137 Jam 2002
[Fic]—dc21
2002022696

ISBN 0-375-81424-8 (trade)
ISBN 0-375-91424-2 (lib. bdg.)

Printed in the United States of America

September 2002

20

Revised Edition

*This book is for
Olivia and Tessa*

1

Until he was four years old, James Henry Trotter had had a happy life. He lived peacefully with his mother and father in a beautiful house beside the sea. There were always plenty of other children for him to play with, and there was the sandy beach for him to run about on, and the ocean to paddle in. It was the perfect life for a small boy.

Then, one day, James's mother and father went to London to do some shopping, and there a terrible thing happened. Both of them suddenly got eaten up (in full daylight, mind you, and on a crowded street) by an enormous angry rhinoceros which had escaped from the London Zoo.

Now this, as you can well imagine, was a rather nasty experience for two such gentle parents. But in the long run it was far nastier for James than it was for them. *Their* troubles were all over in a jiffy. They were dead and gone in thirty-five seconds flat. Poor James, on the other hand, was still very much alive, and all at once he found himself alone and frightened in a vast unfriendly world. The lovely house by the seaside had to be sold immediately, and the little boy, carrying nothing but a small suitcase containing a pair of pajamas and a toothbrush, was sent away to live with his two aunts.

Their names were Aunt Sponge and Aunt Spiker, and I am sorry to say that they were both really horrible people. They were selfish and lazy and cruel, and right from the beginning they started beating poor James for almost no reason at all. They never called him by his real name, but always referred to him as "you disgusting little beast" or "you filthy nuisance" or "you miserable creature," and they certainly never gave him any toys to play with or any picture books to look at. His room was as bare as a prison cell.

They lived—Aunt Sponge, Aunt Spiker, and now James as well—in a queer ramshackle house on the top of a high hill in the south of England. The hill was so high that

from almost anywhere in the garden James could look down and see for miles and miles across a marvelous landscape of woods and fields; and on a very clear day, if he looked in the right direction, he could see a tiny gray dot far away on the horizon, which was the house that he used to live in with his beloved mother and father. And just beyond that, he could see the ocean itself—a long thin streak of blackish-blue, like a line of ink, beneath the rim of the sky.

But James was never allowed to go down off the top of that hill. Neither Aunt Sponge nor Aunt Spiker could ever be bothered to take him out herself, not even for a

small walk or a picnic, and he certainly wasn't permitted to go alone. "The nasty little beast will only get into mischief if he goes out of the garden," Aunt Spiker had said. And terrible punishments were promised him, such as being locked up in the cellar with the rats for a week, if he even so much as dared to climb over the fence.

The garden, which covered the whole of the top of the hill, was large and desolate, and the only tree in the entire place (apart from a clump of dirty old laurel bushes at the far end) was an ancient peach tree that never gave any peaches. There was no swing, no seesaw, no sand pit, and no other children were ever invited to

come up the hill to play with poor James. There wasn't so much as a dog or a cat around to keep him company. And as time went on, he became sadder and sadder, and more and more lonely, and he used to spend hours every day standing at the bottom of the garden, gazing wistfully at the lovely but forbidden world of woods and fields and ocean that was spread out below him like a magic carpet.

2

After James Henry Trotter had been living with his aunts for three whole years there came a morning when something rather peculiar happened to him. And this thing, which as I say was only *rather* peculiar, soon caused a second thing to happen which was *very* peculiar. And then the *very* peculiar thing, in its own turn, caused a really *fantastically* peculiar thing to occur.

It all started on a blazing hot day in the middle of summer. Aunt Sponge, Aunt Spiker, and James were all out in the garden. James had been put to work, as usual. This time he was chopping wood for the kitchen stove. Aunt Sponge and Aunt Spiker were sitting comfortably in deck-chairs nearby, sipping tall glasses of fizzy lemonade and watching him to see that he didn't stop work for one moment.

Aunt Sponge was enormously fat and very short. She had small piggy eyes, a sunken mouth, and one of those white flabby faces that looked exactly as though it had been boiled. She was like a great white soggy overboiled cabbage. Aunt Spiker, on the other hand, was lean and tall and bony, and she wore steel-rimmed spectacles that fixed onto the end of her nose with a clip. She had a screeching voice and long wet narrow lips, and whenever she got angry or excited, little flecks of spit would come shooting out of her mouth as she talked. And there they sat, these two ghastly hags, sipping their drinks, and every now and again screaming at James to chop faster and faster. They also talked about themselves, each one

saying how beautiful she thought she was. Aunt Sponge had a long-handled mirror on her lap, and she kept picking it up and gazing at her own hideous face.

> "I look and smell," Aunt Sponge declared, "as
>   lovely as a rose!
> Just feast your eyes upon my face, observe my
>   shapely nose!
> Behold my heavenly silky locks!
> And if I take off both my socks
> You'll see my dainty toes."
> "But don't forget," Aunt Spiker cried, "how much
>   your tummy shows!"

> Aunt Sponge went red. Aunt Spiker said, "My
>   sweet, you cannot win,
> Behold MY gorgeous curvy shape, my teeth, my
>   charming grin!
> Oh, beauteous me! How I adore
> My radiant looks! And please ignore
> The pimple on my chin."
> "My dear old trout!" Aunt Sponge cried out,
>   "You're only bones and skin!"

> "Such loveliness as I possess can only truly
>   shine
> In Hollywood!" Aunt Sponge declared. "Oh,
>   wouldn't that be fine!
> I'd capture all the nations' hearts!
> They'd give me all the leading parts!
> The stars would all resign!"

"I think you'd make," Aunt Spiker said, "a lovely Frankenstein."

Poor James was still slaving away at the chopping-block. The heat was terrible. He was sweating all over. His arm was aching. The chopper was a large blunt thing far too heavy for a small boy to use. And as he worked, James began thinking about all the other children in the world and what they might be doing at this moment. Some would be riding tricycles in their gardens. Some would be walking in cool woods and picking bunches of wild flowers. And all the little friends whom he used to know would be down by the seaside, playing in the wet sand and splashing around in the water . . .

Great tears began oozing out of James's eyes and rolling down his cheeks. He stopped working and leaned against the chopping-block, overwhelmed by his own unhappiness.

"What's the matter with you?" Aunt Spiker screeched, glaring at him over the top of her steel spectacles.

James began to cry.

"Stop that immediately and get on with your work, you nasty little beast!" Aunt Sponge ordered.

"Oh, Auntie Sponge!" James cried out. "And Auntie Spiker! Couldn't we all—*please*—just for once—go down to the seaside on the bus? It isn't very far—and I feel so hot and awful and lonely . . ."

"Why, you lazy good-for-nothing brute!" Aunt Spiker shouted.

"Beat him!" cried Aunt Sponge.

"I certainly will!" Aunt Spiker snapped. She glared at James, and James looked back at her with large frightened eyes. "I shall beat you later on in the day when I don't feel so hot," she said. "And now get out of my sight, you disgusting little worm, and give me some peace!"

James turned and ran. He ran off as fast as he could to the far end of the garden and hid himself behind that clump of dirty old laurel bushes that we mentioned earlier on. Then he covered his face with his hands and began to cry and cry.

3

IT WAS AT THIS POINT that the first thing of all, the *rather* peculiar thing that led to so many other *much* more peculiar things, happened to him.

For suddenly, just behind him, James heard a rustling of leaves, and he turned around and saw an old man in a crazy dark-green suit emerging from the bushes. He was a very small old man, but he had a huge bald head and a face that was covered all over with bristly black whiskers. He stopped when he was about three yards away, and he stood there leaning on his stick and staring hard at James.

When he spoke, his voice was very slow and creaky. "Come closer to me, little boy," he said, beckoning to James with a finger. "Come right up close to me and I will show you something *wonderful*."

James was too frightened to move.

The old man hobbled a step or two nearer, and then he put a hand into the pocket of his jacket and took out a small white paper bag.

"You see this?" he whispered, waving the bag gently to and fro in front of James's face. "You know what this is, my dear? You know what's inside this little bag?"

Then he came nearer still, leaning forward and pushing his face so close to James that James could feel breath blowing on his cheeks. The breath smelled musty and stale and slightly mildewed, like air in an old cellar.

"Take a look, my dear," he said, opening the bag and tilting it toward James. Inside it, James could see a mass of tiny green things that looked like little stones or crystals, each one about the size of a grain of rice. They were extraordinarily beautiful, and there was a strange brightness about them, a sort of luminous quality that made them glow and sparkle in the most wonderful way.

"Listen to them!" the old man whispered. "Listen to them move!"

James stared into the bag, and sure enough there was a faint rustling sound coming up from inside it, and then he noticed that all the thousands of little green things were slowly, very very slowly stirring about and moving over each other as though they were alive.

"There's more power and magic in those things in there than in all the rest of the world put together," the old man said softly.

"But—but—what *are* they?" James murmured, finding his voice at last. "Where do they come from?"

"Ah-ha," the old man whispered. "You'd never guess that!" He was crouching a little now and pushing his face still closer and closer to James until the tip of his long nose was actually touching the skin on James's forehead. Then suddenly he jumped back and began waving his stick madly in the air. "Crocodile tongues!" he cried. "One thousand long slimy crocodile tongues boiled up in the skull of a dead witch for twenty days and nights with the eyeballs of a lizard! Add the fingers of a young monkey, the gizzard of a pig, the beak of a green parrot, the juice of a porcupine, and three spoonfuls of sugar. Stew for another week, and then let the moon do the rest!"

All at once, he pushed the white paper bag into James's hands, and said, "Here! You take it! It's yours!"

4

JAMES HENRY TROTTER stood there clutching the bag and staring at the old man.

"And now," the old man said, "all you've got to do is this. Take a large jug of water, and pour all the little green things into it. Then, very slowly, one by one, add ten hairs from your own head. That sets them off! It gets them going! In a couple of minutes the water will begin to froth and bubble furiously, and as soon as that happens you must quickly drink it all down, the whole jugful, in one gulp. And then, my dear, you will feel it churning and boiling in your stomach, and steam will start coming out of your mouth, and immediately after that, *marvelous* things will start happening to you, *fabulous, unbeliev-able* things—and you will never be miserable again in your life. Because you *are* miserable, aren't you? You needn't tell me! I know *all* about it! Now, off you go and do exactly as I say. And don't whisper a word of this to those two horrible aunts of yours! Not a word! And don't let those green things in there get away from you either! Because if they do escape, then they will be working their magic upon somebody else instead of upon *you*! And that isn't what you want at all, is it, my dear? *Whoever they meet first, be it bug, insect, animal, or tree, that will be the one who gets the full power of their magic!* So hold the bag tight! Don't tear the paper! Off you go! Hurry up! Don't wait! Now's the time! Hurry!"

With that, the old man turned away and disappeared into the bushes.

5

THE NEXT MOMENT, James was running back toward the house as fast as he could go. He would do it all in the kitchen, he told himself—if only he could get in there without Aunt Sponge and Aunt Spiker seeing him. He was terribly excited. He flew through the long grass and the stinging-nettles, not caring whether he got stung or not on his bare knees, and in the distance he could see Aunt Sponge and Aunt Spiker sitting in their chairs with their backs toward him. He swerved away from them so as to go around the other side of the house, but then suddenly, just as he was passing underneath the old peach tree that stood in the middle of the garden, his foot slipped and he fell flat on his face in the grass. The paper bag burst open

as it hit the ground and the thousands of tiny green things were scattered in all directions.

James immediately picked himself up onto his hands and knees and started searching around for his precious treasures. *But what was this?* They were all sinking into the soil! He could actually see them wriggling and twisting as they burrowed their way downward into the hard earth, and at once he reached out a hand to pick some of them up before it was too late, but they disappeared right under his fingers. He went after some others, and the same thing happened! He began scrabbling around frantically in an effort to catch hold of those that were left, but they were too quick for him. Each time the tips of his fingers were just about to touch them, they vanished into the earth! And soon, in the space of only a few seconds, every single one of them had gone!

James felt like crying. He would never get them back now—they were lost, lost, lost forever.

But where had they gone to? And why in the world had they been so eager to push down into the earth like that? What were they after? There was nothing down *there*. Nothing except the roots of the old peach tree . . . and a whole lot of earthworms and centipedes and insects living in the soil.

But what was it that the old man had said? *Whoever they meet first, be it bug, insect, animal, or tree, that will be the one who gets the full power of their magic!*

Good heavens, thought James. What is going to happen in that case if they *do* meet an earthworm? Or a centipede? Or a spider? And what if they *do* go into the roots of the peach tree?

"Get up at once, you lazy little beast!" a voice was suddenly shouting in James's ear. James glanced up and saw Aunt Spiker standing over him, grim and tall and bony, glaring at him through her steel-rimmed spectacles. "Get back over there immediately and finish chopping up those logs!" she ordered.

Aunt Sponge, fat and pulpy as a jellyfish, came waddling up behind her sister to see what was going on. "Why don't we just lower the boy down the well in a bucket and leave him there for the night?" she suggested. "That ought to teach him not to laze around like this the whole day long."

"That's a very good wheeze, my dear Sponge. But let's make him finish chopping up the wood first. Be off with you at once, you hideous brat, and do some work!"

Slowly, sadly, poor James got up off the ground and went back to the woodpile. Oh, if only he hadn't slipped and fallen and dropped that precious bag. All hope of a happier life had gone completely now. Today and tomorrow and the next day and all the other days as well would be nothing but punishment and pain, unhappiness and despair.

He picked up the chopper and was just about to start chopping away again when he heard a shout behind him that made him stop and turn.

6

"Sponge! Sponge! Come here at once and look at this!"

"At what?"

"It's a peach!" Aunt Spiker was shouting.

"A what?"

"A peach! Right up there on the highest branch! Can't you see it?"

"I think you must be mistaken, my dear Spiker. That miserable tree *never* has any peaches on it."

"There's one on it now, Sponge! You look for yourself!"

"You're teasing me, Spiker. You're making my mouth

water on purpose when there's nothing to put into it. Why, that tree's never even had a *blossom* on it, let alone a peach. Right up on the highest branch, you say? I can't see a thing. Very funny . . . Ha, ha . . . *Good gracious* me! Well, *I'll be blowed!* There really *is* a peach up there!"

"A nice big one, too!" Aunt Spiker said.

"A beauty, a beauty!" Aunt Sponge cried out.

At this point, James slowly put down his chopper and turned and looked across at the two women, who were standing underneath the peach tree.

Something is about to happen, he told himself. *Something peculiar is about to happen any moment.* He hadn't the faintest idea what it might be, but he could feel it in his bones that something was going to happen soon. He could feel it in the air around him . . . in the sudden stillness that had fallen upon the garden. . . .

James tiptoed a little closer to the tree. The aunts were not talking now. They were just standing there, staring at the peach. There was not a sound anywhere, not even a breath of wind, and overhead the sun blazed down upon them out of a deep blue sky.

"It looks ripe to me," Aunt Spiker said, breaking the silence.

"Then why don't we eat it?" Aunt Sponge suggested, licking her thick lips. "We can have half each. Hey, you! James! Come over here at once and climb this tree!"

James came running over.

"I want you to pick that peach up there on the highest branch," Aunt Sponge went on. "Can you see it?"

"Yes, Auntie Sponge, I can see it!"

"And don't you dare to eat any of it yourself. Your Aunt Spiker and I are going to have it between us right here and now, half each. Get on with you! Up you go!"

James crossed over to the tree trunk.

"Stop!" Aunt Spiker said quickly. "Hold everything!" She was staring up into the branches with her mouth wide open and her eyes bulging as though she had seen a ghost. *"Look!"* she said. *"Look,* Sponge, *look!"*

"What's the matter with you?" Aunt Sponge demanded.

"It's *growing*!" Aunt Spiker cried. "It's getting bigger and bigger!"

"What is?"

"The peach, of course!"

"You're joking!"

"Well, look for yourself!"

"But my dear Spiker, that's perfectly ridiculous. That's impossible. That's—that's—that's—Now, wait *just* a minute—No—No—that can't be right—No—Yes—Great Scott! The thing really *is* growing!"

"It's nearly twice as big already!" Aunt Spiker shouted.

"It can't be true!"

"It *is* true!"

"It must be a miracle!"

"Watch it! Watch it!"

"I *am* watching it!"

"Great Heavens alive!" Aunt Spiker yelled. "I can actually see the thing bulging and swelling before my very eyes!"

7

THE TWO WOMEN and the small boy stood absolutely still on the grass underneath the tree, gazing up at this extraordinary fruit. James's little face was glowing with excitement, his eyes were as big and bright as two stars. He could see the peach swelling larger and larger as clearly as if it were a balloon being blown up.

In half a minute, it was the size of a melon!

In another half-minute, it was *twice* as big again!

"Just *look* at it growing!" Aunt Spiker cried.

"Will it ever stop!" Aunt Sponge shouted, waving her fat arms and starting to dance around in circles.

And now it was so big it looked like an enormous butter-colored pumpkin dangling from the top of the tree.

"Get away from that tree trunk, you stupid boy!" Aunt Spiker yelled. "The slightest shake and I'm sure it'll fall off! It must weigh twenty or thirty pounds at least!"

The branch that the peach was growing upon was beginning to bend over further and further because of the weight.

"Stand back!" Aunt Sponge shouted. "It's coming down! The branch is going to break!"

But the branch didn't break. It simply bent over more and more as the peach got heavier and heavier.

And still it went on growing.

In another minute, this mammoth fruit was as large and round and fat as Aunt Sponge herself, and probably just as heavy.

"It *has* to stop now!" Aunt Spiker yelled. "It can't go on forever!"

But it didn't stop.

Soon it was the size of a small car, and reached halfway to the ground.

Both aunts were now hopping around and around the tree, clapping their hands and shouting all sorts of silly things in their excitement.

"Hallelujah!" Aunt Spiker shouted. "What a peach! What a peach!"

"Terrifico!" Aunt Sponge cried out, "Magnifico! Splendifico! And what a meal!"

"It's still growing!"

"I know! I know!"

As for James, he was so spellbound by the whole thing that he could only stand and stare and murmur quietly to himself, "Oh, isn't it beautiful. It's the most beautiful thing I've ever seen."

"Shut up, you little twerp!" Aunt Spiker snapped, happening to overhear him. "It's none of your business!"

"That's right," Aunt Sponge declared. "It's got nothing to do with you whatsoever! Keep out of it!"

"Look!" Aunt Spiker shouted. "It's growing faster than ever now! It's speeding up!"

"I see it, Spiker! I do! I do!"

Bigger and bigger grew the peach, bigger and bigger and bigger.

Then at last, when it had become nearly as tall as the tree that it was growing on, as tall and wide, in fact, as a small house, the bottom part of it gently touched the ground—and there it rested.

"It can't fall off now!" Aunt Sponge shouted.

"It's stopped growing!" Aunt Spiker cried.

"No, it hasn't!"

"Yes, it has!"

"It's slowing down, Spiker, it's slowing down! But it hasn't stopped yet! You watch it!"

There was a pause.

"It has now!"

"I believe you're right."

"Do you think it's safe to touch it?"

"I don't know. We'd better be careful."

Aunt Sponge and Aunt Spiker began walking slowly around the peach, inspecting it very cautiously from all sides. They were like a couple of hunters who had just shot an elephant and were not quite sure whether it was dead or alive. And the massive round fruit towered over them so high that they looked like midgets from another world beside it.

The skin of the peach was very beautiful—a rich buttery yellow with patches of brilliant pink and red. Aunt Sponge advanced cautiously and touched it with the tip of one finger. "It's ripe!" she cried. "It's just perfect! Now, see here, Spiker. Why don't we go and get us a shovel right away and dig out a great big hunk of it for you and me to eat?"

"No," Aunt Spiker said. "Not yet."

"Whyever not?"

"Because I say so."

"But I can't *wait* to eat some!" Aunt Sponge cried out. She was watering at the mouth now and a thin trickle of spit was running down one side of her chin.

"My dear Sponge," Aunt Spiker said slowly, winking at her sister and smiling a sly, thin-lipped smile. "There's a pile of money to be made out of this if only we can handle it right. You wait and see."

8

THE NEWS THAT A PEACH almost as big as a house had suddenly appeared in someone's garden spread like wildfire across the countryside, and the next day a stream of people came scrambling up the steep hill to gaze upon this marvel.

Quickly, Aunt Sponge and Aunt Spiker called in carpenters and had them build a strong fence around the peach to save it from the crowd; and at the same time, these two crafty women stationed themselves at the front gate with a large bunch of tickets and started charging everyone for coming in.

"Roll up! Roll up!" Aunt Spiker yelled. "Only one shilling to see the giant peach!"

"Half price for children under six weeks old!" Aunt Sponge shouted.

"One at a time, please! Don't push! Don't push! You're all going to get in!"

"Hey, you! Come back, there! You haven't paid!"

By lunchtime, the whole place was a seething mass of men, women, and children all pushing and shoving to get a glimpse of this miraculous fruit. Helicopters were land-

ing like wasps all over the hill, and out of them poured swarms of newspaper reporters, cameramen, and men from the television companies.

"It'll cost you double to bring in a camera!" Aunt Spiker shouted.

"All right! All right!" they answered. "We don't care!" And the money came rolling into the pockets of the two greedy aunts.

But while all this excitement was going on outside, poor James was forced to stay locked in his bedroom, peeping through the bars of his window at the crowds below.

"The disgusting little brute will only get in everyone's way if we let him wander about," Aunt Spiker had said early that morning.

"Oh, *please!*" he had begged. "I haven't met any other children for years and years and there are going to be lots of them down there for me to play with. And perhaps I could help you with the tickets."

"Cut it out!" Aunt Sponge had snapped. "Your Aunt Spiker and I are about to become millionaires, and the last thing we want is the likes of you messing things up and getting in the way."

Later, when the evening of the first day came and the people had all gone home, the aunts unlocked James's door and ordered him to go outside and pick up all the banana skins and orange peel and bits of paper that the crowd had left behind.

"Could I please have something to eat first?" he asked. "I haven't had a thing all day."

"No!" they shouted, kicking him out the door. "We're too busy to make food! We are counting our money!"

"But it's dark!" cried James.

"Get out!" they yelled. "And stay out until you've cleaned up all the mess!" The door slammed. The key turned in the lock.

9

HUNGRY AND TREMBLING, James stood alone out in the open, wondering what to do. The night was all around him now, and high overhead a wild white moon was riding in the sky. There was not a sound, not a movement anywhere.

Most people—and especially small children—are often quite scared of being out of doors alone in the moonlight. Everything is so deadly quiet, and the shadows are so long and black, and they keep turning into strange shapes that seem to move as you look at them, and the slightest little snap of a twig makes you jump.

James felt exactly like that now. He stared straight ahead with large frightened eyes, hardly daring to breathe. Not far away, in the middle of the garden, he could see the giant peach towering over everything else. Surely it was even bigger tonight than ever before? And what a dazzling sight it was! The moonlight was shining and glinting on its great curving sides, turning them to crystal and silver. It looked like a tremendous silver ball lying there in the grass, silent, mysterious, and wonderful.

And then all at once, little shivers of excitement started running over the skin on James's back.

Something else, he told himself, *something stranger than ever this time, is about to happen to me again soon.* He was sure of it. He could feel it coming.

He looked around him, wondering what on earth it was going to be. The garden lay soft and silver in the moonlight. The grass was wet with dew and a million dewdrops were sparkling and twinkling like diamonds around his feet. And now suddenly, the whole place, the whole garden, seemed to be *alive* with magic.

Almost without knowing what he was doing, as though drawn by some powerful magnet, James Henry Trotter started walking slowly toward the giant peach. He climbed over the fence that surrounded it, and stood directly beneath it, staring up at its great bulging sides. He put out a hand and touched it gently with the tip of one finger. It felt soft and warm and slightly furry, like the skin of a baby mouse. He moved a step closer and rubbed his cheek lightly against the soft skin. And then suddenly, while he was doing this, he happened to notice that right beside him and below him, close to the ground, there was a hole in the side of the peach.

10

IT WAS QUITE a large hole, the sort of thing an animal about the size of a fox might have made.

James knelt down in front of it and poked his head and shoulders inside.

He crawled in.

He kept on crawling.

This isn't just a hole, he thought excitedly. *It's a tunnel!*

The tunnel was damp and murky, and all around him there was the curious bittersweet smell of fresh peach. The floor was soggy under his knees, the walls were wet and sticky, and peach juice was dripping from the ceiling. James opened his mouth and caught some of it on his tongue. It tasted delicious.

He was crawling uphill now, as though the tunnel were leading straight toward the very center of the gigantic fruit. Every few seconds he paused and took a bite out of the wall. The peach flesh was sweet and juicy, and marvelously refreshing.

He crawled on for several more yards, and then suddenly—*bang*—the top of his head bumped into something extremely hard blocking his way. He glanced up. In front of him there was a solid wall that seemed at first as though it were made of wood. He touched it with his fingers. It certainly felt like wood, except that it was very jagged and full of deep grooves.

"Good heavens!" he said. "I know what this is! I've come to the stone in the middle of the peach!"

Then he noticed that there was a small door cut into the face of the peach stone. He gave a push. It swung open. He crawled through it, and before he had time to glance up and see where he was, he heard a voice saying, "*Look* who's here!" And another one said, "We've been *waiting* for you!"

James stopped and stared at the speakers, his face white with horror.

He started to stand up, but his knees were shaking so much he had to sit down again on the floor. He glanced behind him, thinking he could bolt back into the tunnel the way he had come, but the doorway had disappeared. There was now only a solid brown wall behind him.

11

JAMES'S LARGE FRIGHTENED EYES traveled slowly around the room.

The creatures, some sitting on chairs, others reclining on a sofa, were all watching him intently.

Creatures?

Or were they insects?

An insect is usually something rather small, is it not? A grasshopper, for example, is an insect.

So what would you call it if you saw a grasshopper as

large as a dog? As large as a *large* dog. You could hardly call *that* an insect, could you?

There was an Old-Green-Grasshopper as large as a large dog sitting on a stool directly across the room from James now.

And next to the Old-Green-Grasshopper, there was an enormous Spider.

And next to the Spider, there was a giant Ladybug with nine black spots on her scarlet shell.

Each of these three was squatting upon a magnificent chair.

On a sofa nearby, reclining comfortably in curled-up positions, there was a Centipede and an Earthworm.

On the floor over in the far corner, there was something thick and white that looked as though it might be a

Silkworm. But it was sleeping soundly and nobody was paying any attention to it.

Every one of these "creatures" was at least as big as James himself, and in the strange greenish light that shone down from somewhere in the ceiling, they were absolutely terrifying to behold.

"I'm hungry!" the Spider announced suddenly, staring hard at James.

"*I'm* famished!" the Old-Green-Grasshopper said.

"So am *I*!" the Ladybug cried.

The Centipede sat up a little straighter on the sofa. "*Everyone's* famished!" he said. "We need food!"

Four pairs of round black glassy eyes were all fixed upon James.

The Centipede made a wriggling movement with his body as though he were about to glide off the sofa—but he didn't.

There was a long pause—and a long silence.

The Spider (who happened to be a female spider) opened her mouth and ran a long black tongue delicately over her lips. "Aren't *you* hungry?" she asked suddenly, leaning forward and addressing herself to James.

Poor James was backed up against the far wall, shivering with fright and much too terrified to answer.

"What's the matter with you?" the Old-Green-Grasshopper asked. "You look positively ill!"

"He looks as though he's going to faint any second," the Centipede said.

"Oh, my goodness, the poor thing!" the Ladybug cried. "I do believe he thinks it's *him* that we are wanting to eat!"

There was a roar of laughter from all sides.

"Oh dear, oh dear!" they said. "What an awful thought!"

"You mustn't be frightened," the Ladybug said kindly. "We wouldn't *dream* of hurting you. You are one of *us* now, didn't you know that? You are one of the crew. We're all in the same boat."

"We've been waiting for you all day long," the Old-Green-Grasshopper said. "We thought you were never going to turn up. I'm glad you made it."

"So cheer up, my boy, cheer up!" the Centipede said. "And meanwhile I wish you'd come over here and give me a hand with these boots. It takes me *hours* to get them all off by myself."

12

JAMES DECIDED that this was most certainly not a time to be disagreeable, so he crossed the room to where the Centipede was sitting and knelt down beside him.

"Thank you so much," the Centipede said. "You are very kind."

"You have a lot of boots," James murmured.

"I have a lot of legs," the Centipede answered proudly. "And a lot of feet. One hundred, to be exact."

"*There* he goes again!" the Earthworm cried, speaking for the first time. "He simply cannot stop telling lies about his legs! He doesn't have anything *like* a hundred of them! He's only got forty-two! The trouble is that most people don't bother to count them. They just take his word.

And anyway, there is nothing *marvelous*, you know, Centipede, about having a lot of legs."

"Poor fellow," the Centipede said, whispering in James's ear. "He's blind. He can't see how splendid I look."

"In my opinion," the Earthworm said, "the *really* mar-

velous thing is to have no legs at all and to be able to walk just the same."

"You call that *walking*!" cried the Centipede. "You're a *slitherer*, that's all you are! You just *slither* along!"

"I glide," said the Earthworm primly.

"You are a slimy beast," answered the Centipede.

"I am *not* a slimy beast," the Earthworm said. "I am a useful and much loved creature. Ask any gardener you like. And as for you . . ."

"I am a pest!" the Centipede announced, grinning broadly and looking round the room for approval.

"He is *so* proud of that," the Ladybug said, smiling at James. "Though for the life of me I cannot understand why."

"I am the only pest in this room!" cried the Centipede, still grinning away. "Unless you count Old-Green-Grasshopper over there. But he is long past it now. He is too old to be a pest any more."

The Old-Green-Grasshopper turned his huge black eyes upon the Centipede and gave him a withering look. "Young fellow," he said, speaking in a deep, slow, scornful voice, "I have never been a pest in my life. I am a musician."

"Hear, hear!" said the Ladybug.

"James," the Centipede said. "Your names *is* James, isn't it?"

"Yes."

"Well, James, have you ever in your life seen such a marvelous colossal Centipede as me?"

"I certainly haven't," James answered. "How on earth did you get to be like that?"

"*Very* peculiar," the Centipede said. "*Very, very* peculiar indeed. Let me tell you what happened. I was messing about in the garden under the old peach tree and suddenly a funny little green thing came wriggling past my nose. Bright green it was, and extraordinarily beautiful, and it looked like some kind of a tiny stone or crystal . . ."

"Oh, but I know what that was!" cried James.

"It happened to me, too!" said the Ladybug.

"And me!" Miss Spider said. "Suddenly there were little green things everywhere! The soil was full of them!"

"I actually swallowed one!" the Earthworm declared proudly.

"So did I!" the Ladybug said.

"I swallowed three!" the Centipede cried. "But who's telling this story anyway? Don't interrupt!"

"It's too late to tell stories now," the Old-Green-Grasshopper announced. "It's time to go to sleep."

"I refuse to sleep in my boots!" the Centipede cried. "How many more are there to come off, James?"

"I think I've done about twenty so far," James told him.

"Then that leaves eighty to go," the Centipede said.

"*Twenty-two*, not *eighty*!" shrieked the Earthworm. "He's lying again."

The Centipede roared with laughter.

"Stop pulling the Earthworm's leg," the Ladybug said.

This sent the Centipede into hysterics. "Pulling his *leg*!" he cried, wriggling with glee and pointing at the Earthworm. "Which leg am I pulling? You tell me that?"

James decided that he rather liked the Centipede. He was obviously a rascal, but what a change it was to hear somebody laughing once in a while. He had never heard Aunt Sponge or Aunt Spiker laughing aloud in all the time he had been with them.

"We really *must* get some sleep," the Old-Green-Grasshopper said. "We've got a tough day ahead of us tomorrow. So would you be kind enough, Miss Spider, to make the beds?"

13

A FEW MINUTES LATER, Miss Spider had made the first bed. It was hanging from the ceiling, suspended by a rope of threads at either end so that actually it looked more like a hammock than a bed. But it was a magnificent affair, and the stuff that it was made of shimmered like silk in the pale light.

"I do hope you'll find it comfortable," Miss Spider said to the Old-Green-Grasshopper. "I made it as soft and silky as I possibly could. I spun it with gossamer. That's a much better quality thread than the one I use for my own web."

"Thank you so much, my dear lady," the Old-Green-Grasshopper said, climbing into the hammock. "Ah, this is just what I needed. Good night, everybody. Good night."

Then Miss Spider spun the next hammock, and the Ladybug got in.

After that, she spun a long one for the Centipede, and an even longer one for the Earthworm.

"And how do you like *your* bed?" she said to James when it came to his turn. "Hard or soft?"

"I like it soft, thank you very much," James answered.

"For goodness' sake stop staring round the room and

get on with my boots!" the Centipede said. "You and I are never going to get any sleep at this rate! And kindly line them up neatly in pairs as you take them off. Don't just throw them over your shoulder."

James worked away frantically on the Centipede's boots. Each one had laces that had to be untied and loosened before it could be pulled off, and to make matters worse, all the laces were tied up in the most complicated knots that had to be unpicked with fingernails. It was just awful. It took about two hours. And by the time James had pulled off the last boot of all and had lined them up in a row on the floor—twenty-one pairs altogether—the Centipede was fast asleep.

"Wake up, Centipede," whispered James, giving him a gentle dig in the stomach. "It's time for bed."

"Thank you, my dear child," the Centipede said, opening his eyes. Then he got down off the sofa and ambled across the room and crawled into his hammock. James got into his own hammock—and oh, how soft and comfortable it was compared with the hard bare boards that his aunts had always made him sleep upon at home.

"Lights out," said the Centipede drowsily.

Nothing happened.

"Turn out the light!" he called, raising his voice.

James glanced round the room, wondering which of the others he might be talking to, but they were all asleep. The Old-Green-Grasshopper was snoring loudly through his nose. The Ladybug was making whistling noises as she breathed, and the Earthworm was coiled up like a spring at one end of his hammock, wheezing and blowing through his open mouth. As for Miss Spider, she had made a lovely web for herself across one corner of the room, and James could see her crouching right in the very center of it, mumbling softly in her dreams.

"I said turn out the light!" shouted the Centipede angrily.

"Are you talking to me?" James asked him.

"Of course I'm not talking to you, you ass!" the Centipede answered. "That crazy Glow-worm has gone to sleep with her light on!"

For the first time since entering the room, James glanced up at the ceiling—and there he saw a most extraordinary sight. Something that looked like a gigantic fly without wings (it was at least three feet long) was standing upside down upon its six legs in the middle of the ceiling, and the tail end of this creature seemed to be literally on fire. A brilliant greenish light as bright as the brightest electric bulb was shining out of its tail and lighting up the whole room.

"Is *that* a Glow-worm?" asked James, staring at the light. "It doesn't look like a worm of any sort to me."

"Of course it's a Glow-worm," the Centipede answered. "At least that's what *she* calls herself. Although actually you are quite right. She isn't really a worm at all. Glow-worms are never worms. They are simply lady fireflies without wings. Wake up, you lazy beast!"

But the Glow-worm didn't stir, so the Centipede reached out of his hammock and picked up one of his boots from the floor. "Put out that wretched light!" he shouted, hurling the boot up at the ceiling.

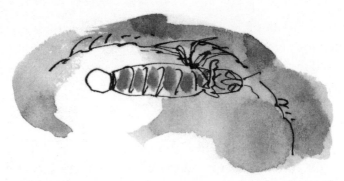

The Glow-worm slowly opened one eye and stared at the Centipede. "There is no need to be rude," she said coldly. "All in good time."

"Come on, come on, come on!" shouted the Centipede. "Or I'll put it out for you!"

"Oh, hello, James!" the Glow-worm said, looking down and giving James a little wave and a smile. "I didn't see you come in. Welcome, my dear boy, welcome—and good night!"

Then *click*—and out went the light.

James Henry Trotter lay there in the darkness with his eyes wide open, listening to the strange sleeping noises that the "creatures" were making all around him, and wondering what on earth was going to happen to him in the morning. Already, he was beginning to like his new friends very much. They were not nearly as terrible as they looked. In fact, they weren't really terrible at all. They seemed extremely kind and helpful in spite of all the shouting and arguing that went on between them.

"Good night, Old-Green-Grasshopper," he whispered. "Good night, Ladybug—Good night, Miss Spider—" But before he could go through them all, he had fallen fast asleep.

14

"WE'RE OFF!" someone was shouting. "We're off at last!"

James woke up with a jump and looked about him. The creatures were all out of their hammocks and moving excitedly around the room. Suddenly the floor gave a great heave, as though an earthquake were taking place.

"Here we go!" shouted the Old-Green-Grasshopper, hopping up and down with excitement. "Hold on tight!"

"What's happening?" cried James, leaping out of his hammock. "What's going on?"

The Ladybug, who was obviously a kind and gentle creature, came over and stood beside him. "In case you don't know it," she said, "we are about to depart forever from the top of this ghastly hill that we've all been living on for so long. We are about to roll away inside this great big beautiful peach to a land of . . . of . . . of . . . to a land of—"

"Of what?" asked James.

"Never you mind," said the Ladybug. "But nothing could be worse than this desolate hilltop and those two repulsive aunts of yours—"

"Hear, hear!" they all shouted. "Hear, hear!"

"You may not have noticed it," the Ladybug went on, "but the whole garden, even before it reaches the steep edge of the hill, happens to be on a steep slope. And therefore the only thing that has been stopping this peach from rolling away right from the beginning is the thick stem attaching it to the tree. Break the stem, and off we go!"

"Watch it!" cried Miss Spider, as the room gave another violent lurch. "Here we go!"

"Not quite! Not quite!"

"At this moment," continued the Ladybug, "our Centipede, who has a pair of jaws as sharp as razors, is up there on top of the peach nibbling away at that stem. In fact, he must be nearly through it, as you can tell from the way we're lurching about. Would you like me to take you under my wing so that you won't fall over when we start rolling?"

"That's very kind of you," said James, "but I think I'll be all right."

Just then, the Centipede stuck his grinning face through a hole in the ceiling and shouted, "I've done it! We're off!"

"We're off!" the others cried. "We're off!"

"The journey begins!" shouted the Centipede.

"And who knows where it will end," muttered the Earthworm, "if *you* have anything to do with it. It can only mean trouble."

"Nonsense," said the Ladybug. "We are now about to visit the most marvelous places and see the most wonderful things! Isn't that so, Centipede?"

"There is no knowing what we shall see!" cried the Centipede.

> *"We may see a Creature with forty-nine*
>   *heads*
> *Who lives in the desolate snow,*
> *And whenever he catches a cold (which he*
>   *dreads)*
> *He has forty-nine noses to blow.*

> *"We may see the venomous Pink-Spotted*
>   *Scrunch*
> *Who can chew up a man with one bite.*
> *It likes to eat five of them roasted for lunch*
> *And eighteen for its supper at night.*

"We may see a Dragon, and nobody knows
That we won't see a Unicorn there.
We may see a terrible Monster with toes
Growing out of the tufts of his hair.

"We may see the sweet little Biddy-Bright Hen
So playful, so kind and well-bred;
And such beautiful eggs! You just boil them
 and then
They explode and they blow off your head.

"A Gnu and a Gnocerous surely you'll see
And that gnormous and gnorrible Gnat
Whose sting when it stings you goes in at
 the knee
And comes out through the top of your hat.

"We may even get lost and be frozen by frost.
We may die in an earthquake or tremor.
Or nastier still, we may even be tossed
On the horns of a furious Dilemma.

"But who cares! Let us go from this horrible
 hill!
Let us roll! Let us bowl! Let us plunge!
Let's go rolling and bowling and spinning until
We're away from old Spiker and Sponge!"

One second later . . . slowly, insidiously, oh most gently,
the great peach started to lean forward and steal into
motion. The whole room began to tilt over and all the fur-

niture went sliding across the floor, and crashed against the far wall. So did James and the Ladybug and the Old-Green-Grasshopper and Miss Spider and the Earthworm, also the Centipede, who had just come slithering quickly down the wall.

15

OUTSIDE IN THE GARDEN, at that very moment, Aunt Sponge and Aunt Spiker had just taken their places at the front gate, each with a bunch of tickets in her hand, and the first stream of early-morning sightseers was visible in the distance climbing up the hill to view the peach.

"We shall make a fortune today," Aunt Spiker was saying. "Just look at all those people!"

"I wonder what became of that horrid little boy of ours last night," Aunt Sponge said. "He never did come back in, did he?"

"He probably fell down in the dark and broke his leg," Aunt Spiker said.

"Or his neck, maybe," Aunt Sponge said hopefully.

"Just *wait* till I get my hands on him," Aunt Spiker said, waving her cane. "He'll never want to stay out all night again by the time *I've* finished with him. Good gracious me! What's that awful noise?"

Both women swung around to look.

The noise, of course, had been caused by the giant peach crashing through the fence that surrounded it, and

now, gathering speed every second, it came rolling across
the garden toward the place where Aunt Sponge and
Aunt Spiker were standing.

They gaped. They screamed. They started to run. They
panicked. They both got in each other's way. They began
pushing and jostling, and each of them was thinking only

about saving herself. Aunt Sponge, the fat one, tripped over a box that she'd brought along to keep the money in, and fell flat on her face. Aunt Spiker immediately tripped over Aunt Sponge and came down on top of her. They both lay on the ground, fighting and clawing and yelling and struggling frantically to get up again, but before they could do this, the mighty peach was upon them.

There was a crunch.

And then there was silence.

The peach rolled on. And behind it, Aunt Sponge and Aunt Spiker lay ironed out upon the grass as flat and thin and lifeless as a couple of paper dolls cut out of a picture book.

16

AND NOW THE PEACH had broken out of the garden and was over the edge of the hill, rolling and bouncing down the steep slope at a terrific pace. Faster and faster and faster it went, and the crowds of people who were climbing up the hill suddenly caught sight of this terrible monster plunging down upon them and they screamed and scattered to right and left as it went hurtling by.

At the bottom of the hill it charged across the road, knocking over a telegraph pole and flattening two parked automobiles as it went by.

Then it rushed madly across about twenty fields, breaking down all the fences and hedges in its path. It went right through the middle of a herd of fine Jersey cows, and then through a flock of sheep, and then through a paddock full of horses, and then through a yard full of pigs, and soon the whole countryside was a seething mass of panic-stricken animals stampeding in all directions.

The peach was still going at a tremendous speed with no sign of slowing down, and about a mile farther on it came to a village.

Down the main street of the village it rolled, with people leaping frantically out of its path right and left, and at the end of the street it went crashing right through the wall of an enormous building and out the other side, leaving two gaping round holes in the brickwork.

This building happened to be a famous factory where they made chocolate, and almost at once a great river of warm melted chocolate came pouring out of the holes in the factory wall. A minute later, this brown sticky mess was flowing through every street in the village, oozing under the doors of houses and into people's shops and gardens. Children were wading in it up to their knees, and some were even trying to swim in it, and all of them were sucking it into their mouths in great greedy gulps and shrieking with joy.

But the peach rushed on across the countryside—on and on and on, leaving a trail of destruction in its wake. Cowsheds, stables, pigsties, barns, bungalows, hayricks, anything that got in its way went toppling over like a nine-pin. An old man sitting quietly beside a stream had his fishing rod whisked out of his hands as it went dashing by, and a woman called Daisy Entwistle was standing so close to it as it passed that she had the skin taken off the tip of her long nose.

Would it ever stop?

Why should it? A round object will always keep on rolling as long as it is on a downhill slope, and in this case the land sloped downhill all the way until it reached the ocean—the same ocean that James had begged his aunts to be allowed to visit the day before.

Well, perhaps he was going to visit it now. The peach was rushing closer and closer to it every second, and closer also to the towering white cliffs that came first.

These cliffs are the most famous in the whole of England, and they are hundreds of feet high. Below them, the sea is deep and cold and hungry. Many ships have been swallowed up and lost forever on this part of the coast, and all the men who were in them as well. The peach was now only a hundred yards away from the cliff—now fifty—now twenty—now ten—now five—and when it reached the edge of the cliff it seemed to leap up into the sky and hang there suspended for a few seconds, still turning over and over in the air . . .

Then it began to fall . . .

Down . . .

Down . . .

Down . . .

Down . . .

Down . . .

SMACK! It hit the water with a colossal splash and sank like a stone.

But a few seconds later, up it came again, and this time, up it stayed, floating serenely upon the surface of the water.

17

AT THIS MOMENT, the scene inside the peach itself was one of indescribable chaos. James Henry Trotter was lying bruised and battered on the floor of the room amongst a tangled mass of Centipede and Earthworm and Spider and Ladybug and Glow-worm and Old-Green-Grasshopper. In the whole history of the world, no travelers had ever had a more terrible journey than these unfortunate creatures. It had started out well, with much laughing and shouting, and for the first few seconds, as the peach had begun to roll slowly forward, nobody had minded being tumbled about a little bit. And when it went *BUMP!* and the Centipede had shouted, "*That* was Aunt Sponge!" and then *BUMP!* again, and "*That* was Aunt Spiker!" there had been a tremendous burst of cheering all around.

But as soon as the peach rolled out of the garden and began to go down the steep hill, rushing and plunging and bounding madly downward, then the whole thing became a nightmare. James found himself being flung up against the ceiling, then back onto the floor, then sideways against the wall, then up onto the ceiling again, and up and down and back and forth and round and round, and at the same time all the other creatures were flying through the air in every direction, and so were the chairs and the sofa, not to mention the forty-two boots belonging to the Centipede. Everything and all of them were being rattled around like peas inside an enormous rattle that was being rattled by a mad giant who refused to stop. To make it worse, something went wrong with the Glow-worm's lighting system, and the room was in pitchy darkness. There were screams and yells and curses and cries of pain, and everything kept going round and round, and once James made a frantic grab at some thick bars sticking out from the wall only to find that they were a couple of the Centipede's legs. "Let go, you idiot!" shouted the Centipede, kicking himself free, and James was promptly flung across the room into the Old-Green-Grasshopper's horny lap. Twice he got tangled up in Miss Spider's legs (a horrid business), and toward the end, the poor Earthworm, who was cracking himself like a whip every time he flew through the air from one side of the room to the other, coiled himself around James's body in a panic and refused to unwind.

Oh, it was a frantic and terrible trip!

But it was all over now, and the room was suddenly very still and quiet. Everybody was beginning slowly and painfully to disentangle himself from everybody else.

"Let's have some light!" shouted the Centipede.

"Yes!" they cried. "Light! Give us some light!"

"I'm *trying*," answered the poor Glow-worm. "I'm doing my best. Please be patient."

They all waited in silence.

Then a faint greenish light began to glimmer out of the Glow-worm's tail, and this gradually became stronger

and stronger until it was anyway enough to see by.

"*Some great journey!*" the Centipede said, limping across the room.

"I shall *never* be the same again," murmured the Earthworm.

"Nor I," the Ladybug said. "It's taken *years* off my life."

"But my dear friends!" cried the Old-Green-Grasshopper, trying to be cheerful, "we are *there*!"

"Where?" they asked. "Where? Where is *there*?"

"I don't know," the Old-Green-Grasshopper said. "But I'll bet it's somewhere good."

"We are probably at the bottom of a coal mine," the Earthworm said gloomily. "We certainly went down and down and down very suddenly at the last moment. I felt it in my stomach. I still feel it."

"Perhaps we are in the middle of a beautiful country full of songs and music," the Old-Green-Grasshopper said.

"Or near the seashore," said James eagerly, "with lots of other children down on the sand for me to play with!"

"Pardon me," murmured the Ladybug, turning a trifle pale, "but am I wrong in thinking that we seem to be bobbing up and down?"

"*Bobbing* up and down!" they cried. "What on earth do you mean?"

"You're still giddy from the journey," the Old-Green-Grasshopper told her. "You'll get over it in a minute. Is everybody ready to go upstairs now and take a look around?"

"Yes, yes!" they chorused. "Come on! Let's go!"

"I *refuse* to show myself out of doors in my bare feet," the Centipede said. "I have to get my boots on again first."

"For heaven's sake, let's not go through all that nonsense again," the Earthworm said.

"Let's *all* lend the Centipede a hand and get it over with," the Ladybug said. "Come on."

So they did, all except Miss Spider, who set about

weaving a long rope-ladder that would reach from the floor up to a hole in the ceiling. The Old-Green-Grasshopper had wisely said that they must not risk going out of the side entrance when they didn't know where they were, but must first of all go up onto the top of the peach and have a look around.

So half an hour later, when the rope-ladder had been finished and hung, and the forty-second boot had been laced neatly onto the Centipede's forty-second foot, they were all ready to go out. Amidst mounting excitement and shouts of "Here we go, boys! The Promised Land! I can't wait to see it!" the whole company climbed up the ladder one by one and disappeared into a dark soggy tunnel in the ceiling that went steeply, almost vertically upward.

18

A MINUTE LATER, they were out in the open, standing on the very top of the peach, near the stem, blinking their eyes in the strong sunlight and peering nervously around.

"What happened?"

"Where are we?"

"But this is *impossible*!"

"Unbelievable!"

"Terrible!"

"I *told* you we were bobbing up and down," the Ladybug said.

"We're in the middle of the sea!" cried James.

And indeed they were. A strong current and a high wind had carried the peach so quickly away from the shore that already the land was out of sight. All around them lay the vast black ocean, deep and hungry. Little waves were bibbling against the sides of the peach.

"But how did it happen?" they cried. "Where are the fields? Where are the woods? Where is England?" Nobody, not even James, could understand how in the world a thing like this could have come about.

"Ladies and gentlemen," the Old-Green-Grasshopper said, trying very hard to keep the fear and disappointment out of his voice, "I am afraid that we find ourselves in a rather awkward situation."

"Awkward!" cried the Earthworm. "My dear Old Grasshopper, we are finished! Every one of us is about to perish! I may be blind, you know, but that much I can see quite clearly!"

"Off with my boots!" shouted the Centipede. "I cannot swim with my boots on!"

"I can't swim at all!" cried the Ladybug.

"Nor can I," wailed the Glow-worm.

"Nor I!" said Miss Spider. "None of us three girls can swim a single stroke."

"But you won't *have* to swim," said James calmly. "We are floating beautifully. And sooner or later a ship is bound to come along and pick us up."

They all stared at him in amazement.

"Are you quite sure that we are not sinking?" the Ladybug asked.

"Of course I'm sure," answered James. "Go and look for yourselves."

They all ran over to the side of the peach and peered down at the water below.

"The boy is quite right," the Old-Green-Grasshopper said. "We are floating beautifully. Now we must all sit down and keep perfectly calm. Everything will be all right in the end."

"What absolute nonsense!" cried the Earthworm. "Nothing is ever all right in the end, and well you know it!"

"Poor Earthworm," the Ladybug said, whispering in James's ear. "He loves to make everything into a disaster. He hates to be happy. He is only happy when he is gloomy. Now isn't that odd? But then, I suppose just *being* an Earthworm is enough to make a person pretty gloomy, don't you agree?"

"If this peach is not going to sink," the Earthworm was saying, "and if we are not going to be drowned, then every one of us is going to *starve* to death instead. Do you realize that we haven't had a thing to eat since yesterday morning?"

"By golly, he's right!" cried the Centipede. "For once, Earthworm is right!"

"Of course I'm right," the Earthworm said. "And we're not likely to find anything around here either. We shall get thinner and thinner and thirstier and thirstier, and we shall all die a slow and grisly death from starvation. I am dying already. I am slowly shriveling up for want of food. Personally, I would rather drown."

"But good heavens, you must be *blind*!" said James.

"You know very well I'm blind," snapped the Earthworm. "There's no need to rub it in."

"I didn't mean that," said James quickly. "I'm sorry. But can't you *see* that—"

"See?" shouted the poor Earthworm. "How can I see if I am blind?"

James took a deep, slow breath. "Can't you *realize*," he said patiently, "that we have enough food here to last us for weeks and weeks?"

"Where?" they said. "Where?"

"Why, the peach, of course! Our whole ship is made of food!"

"Jumping Jehoshaphat!" they cried. "We never thought of that!"

"My dear James," said the Old-Green-Grasshopper, laying a front leg affectionately on James's shoulder, "I don't

know *what* we'd do without you. You are so clever. Ladies and gentlemen—we are saved again!"

"We are most certainly not!" said the Earthworm. "You must be crazy! You can't eat the ship! It's the only thing that is keeping us up!"

"We shall starve if we don't!" said the Centipede.

"And we shall drown if we do!" cried the Earthworm.

"Oh dear, oh dear," said the Old-Green-Grasshopper. "Now we're worse off than before!"

"Couldn't we just eat a *little* bit of it?" asked Miss Spider. "I am so dreadfully hungry."

"You can eat all you want," James answered. "It would take us weeks and weeks to make any sort of a dent in this enormous peach. Surely you can see that?"

"Good heavens, he's right again!" cried the Old-Green-Grasshopper, clapping his hands. "It would take weeks and weeks! Of course it would! But let's not go making a lot of holes all over the deck. I think we'd better simply scoop it out of that tunnel over there—the one that we've just come up by."

"An excellent idea," said the Ladybug.

"What are you looking so worried about, Earthworm?" the Centipede asked. "What's the problem?"

"The problem is . . ." the Earthworm said, "the problem is . . . well, the problem is that there is no problem!"

Everyone burst out laughing. "Cheer up, Earthworm!" they said. "Come and eat!" And they all went over to the tunnel entrance and began scooping out great chunks of juicy, golden-colored peach flesh.

"Oh, marvelous!" said the Centipede, stuffing it into his mouth.

"*Dee*-licious!" said the Old-Green-Grasshopper.

"Just fabulous!" said the Glow-worm.

"Oh my!" said the Ladybug primly. "What a heavenly taste!" She looked up at James, and she smiled, and James smiled back at her. They sat down on the deck together, both of them chewing away happily. "You know, James," the Ladybug said, "up until this moment, I have never in my life tasted anything except those tiny little green flies that live on rosebushes. They have a perfectly delightful flavor. But this peach is even better."

"Isn't it glorious!" Miss Spider said, coming over to join them. "Personally, I had always thought that a big, juicy, caught-in-the-web bluebottle was the finest dinner in the world—until I tasted this."

"*What* a flavor!" the Centipede cried. "It's terrific! There's nothing like it! There never has been! And I should know because I personally have tasted all the

finest foods in the world!" Whereupon, the Centipede, with his mouth full of peach and with juice running down all over his chin, suddenly burst into song:

"I've eaten many strange and scrumptious
    dishes in my time,
Like jellied gnats and dandyprats and earwigs
    cooked in slime,
And mice with rice—they're really nice
When roasted in their prime.
(But don't forget to sprinkle them with just a
    pinch of grime.)

"I've eaten fresh mudburgers by the greatest
    cooks there are,
And scrambled dregs and stinkbugs' eggs and
    hornets stewed in tar,
And pails of snails and lizards' tails,
And beetles by the jar.
(A beetle is improved by just a splash of
    vinegar.)

"I often eat boiled slobbages. They're grand
    when served beside
Minced doodlebugs and curried slugs. And have
    you ever tried
Mosquitoes' toes and wampfish roes
Most delicately fried?
(The only trouble is they disagree with my
    inside.)

"I'm mad for crispy wasp-stings on a piece of
buttered toast,
And pickled spines of porcupines. And then a
gorgeous roast
Of dragon's flesh, well hung, not fresh—
It costs a buck at most,
(And comes to you in barrels if you order it by
post.)

"I crave the tasty tentacles of octopi for tea,
I like hot-dogs, I LOVE *hot-frogs, and surely*
you'll agree
A plate of soil with engine oil's
A super recipe.
(I hardly need to mention that it's practically
free.)

"For dinner on my birthday shall I tell you
what I chose:
Hot noodles made from poodles on a slice of
garden hose—
And a rather smelly jelly
Made of armadillo's toes.
(The jelly is delicious, but you have to hold
your nose.)

"Now comes," the Centipede declared, "the
burden of my speech:
These foods are rare beyond compare—some
are right out of reach;
But there's no doubt I'd go without

A million plates of each
For one small mite,
One tiny bite
Of this FANTASTIC PEACH!"

Everybody was feeling happy now. The sun was shining brightly out of a soft blue sky and the day was calm. The giant peach, with the sunlight glinting on its side, was like a massive golden ball sailing upon a silver sea.

19

"LOOK!" CRIED THE CENTIPEDE just as they were finishing their meal. "Look at that funny thin black thing gliding through the water over there!"

They all swung around to look.

"There are two of them," said Miss Spider.

"There are *lots* of them!" said the Ladybug.

"What are they?" asked the Earthworm, getting worried.

"They must be some kind of fish," said the Old-Green-Grasshopper. "Perhaps they have come along to say hello."

"They are sharks!" cried the Earthworm. "I'll bet you anything you like that they are sharks and they have come along to eat us up!"

"What absolute rot!" the Centipede said, but his voice seemed suddenly to have become a little shaky, and he wasn't laughing.

"I am *positive* they are sharks!" said the Earthworm. "I just *know* they are sharks!"

And so, in actual fact, did everybody else, but they were too frightened to admit it.

There was a short silence. They all peered down anxiously at the sharks, who were cruising slowly round and round the peach.

"Just assuming that they *are* sharks," the Centipede said, "there still can't possibly be any danger if we stay up here."

But even as he spoke, one of those thin black fins suddenly changed direction and came cutting swiftly through the water right up to the side of the peach itself. The shark paused and stared up at the company with small evil eyes.

"Go away!" they shouted. "Go away, you filthy beast!"

Slowly, almost lazily, the shark opened his mouth (which was big enough to have swallowed a perambulator) and made a lunge at the peach.

They all watched, aghast.

And now, as though at a signal from the leader, all the other sharks came swimming in toward the peach, and they clustered around it and began to attack it furiously. There must have been twenty or thirty of them at least, all pushing and fighting and lashing their tails and churning the water into a froth.

Panic and pandemonium broke out immediately on top of the peach.

"Oh, we are finished now!" cried Miss Spider, wringing her feet. "They will eat up the whole peach and then there'll be nothing left for us to stand on and they'll start on us!"

"She is right!" shouted the Ladybug. "We are lost forever!"

"Oh, I don't want to be eaten!" wailed the Earthworm.

"But they will take me first of all because I am so fat and juicy and I have no bones!"

"Is there *nothing* we can do?" asked the Ladybug, appealing to James. "Surely *you* can think of a way out of this."

Suddenly they were all looking at James.

"Think!" begged Miss Spider. "*Think*, James, *think*!"

"Come on," said the Centipede. "Come on, James. There *must* be *something* we can do."

Their eyes waited upon him, tense, anxious, pathetically hopeful.

20

"There *is* something that I believe we might try," James Henry Trotter said slowly. "I'm not saying it'll work . . ."

"Tell us!" cried the Earthworm. "Tell us quick!"

"We'll try anything you say!" said the Centipede. "But hurry, hurry, hurry!"

"Be quiet and let the boy speak!" said the Ladybug. "Go on, James."

They all moved a little closer to him. There was a longish pause.

"Go *on!*" they cried frantically. "*Go on!*"

And all the time while they were waiting they could hear the sharks threshing around in the water below them. It was enough to make anyone frantic.

"Come on, James," the Ladybug said, coaxing him.

"I . . . I . . . I'm afraid it's no good after all," James murmured, shaking his head. "I'm terribly sorry. I forgot. We don't have any string. We'd need hundreds of yards of string to make this work."

"What sort of string?" asked the Old-Green-Grasshopper sharply.

"Any sort, just so long as it's strong."

"But my dear boy, that's exactly what we do have! We've got all you want!"

"How? Where?"

"The Silkworm!" cried the Old-Green-Grasshopper. "Didn't you ever notice the Silkworm? She's still downstairs! She never moves! She just lies there sleeping all day long, but we can easily wake her up and make her spin!"

"And what about me, may I ask?" said Miss Spider. "I can spin just as well as any Silkworm. What's more, *I* can spin patterns."

"Can you make enough between you?" asked James.

"As much as you want."

"And quickly?"

"Of course! Of course!"

"And would it be strong?"

"The strongest there is! It's as thick as your finger! But why? What are you going to do?"

"I'm going to lift this peach clear out of the water!" James announced firmly.

"You're mad!" cried the Earthworm.

"It's our only chance."

"The boy's crazy!"

"He's joking!"

"Go on, James," the Ladybug said gently. "How are you going to do it?"

"Skyhooks, I suppose," jeered the Centipede.

"Seagulls," James answered calmly. "The place is full of them. Look up there!"

They all looked up and saw a great mass of seagulls wheeling round and round in the sky.

"I'm going to take a long silk string," James went on, "and I'm going to loop one end of it around a seagull's neck. And then I'm going to tie the other end to the stem of the peach." He pointed to the peach stem, which was standing up like a short thick mast in the middle of the deck.

"Then I'm going to get another seagull and do the same thing again, then another and another—"

"Ridiculous!" they shouted.

"Absurd!"

"Poppycock!"

"Balderdash!"

"Madness!"

And the Old-Green-Grasshopper said, "How can a few seagulls lift an enormous thing like this up into the air, and all of us as well? It would take hundreds . . . thousands . . ."

"There is no shortage of seagulls," James answered. "Look for yourself. We'll probably need four hundred, five

hundred, six hundred . . . maybe even a thousand . . . I don't know . . . I shall simply go on hooking them up to the stem until we have enough to lift us. They'll be bound to lift us in the end. It's like balloons. You give someone enough balloons to hold, I mean *really* enough, then up he goes. And a seagull has far more lifting power than a balloon. If only we have the *time* to do it. If only we are not sunk first by those awful sharks. . . ."

"You're absolutely off your head!" said the Earthworm. "How on earth do you propose to get a loop of string around a seagull's neck? I suppose you're going to fly up there yourself and catch it!"

"The boy's dotty!" said the Centipede.

"Let him finish," said the Ladybug. "Go on, James. How *would* you do it?"

"With bait."

"Bait! What sort of bait?"

"With a worm, of course. Seagulls love worms, didn't you know that? And luckily for us, we have here the biggest, fattest, pinkest, juiciest Earthworm in the world."

"You can stop right there!" the Earthworm said sharply. "That's quite enough!"

"Go on," the others said, beginning to grow interested. "Go on!"

"The seagulls have already spotted him," James continued. "That's why there are so many of them circling around. But they daren't come down to get him while all the rest of us are standing here. So this is what—"

"Stop!" cried the Earthworm. "Stop, stop, stop! I won't have it! I refuse! I—I—I—I—"

"Be quiet!" said the Centipede. "Mind your own business!"

"I like that!"

"My dear Earthworm, you're going to be eaten anyway, so what difference does it make whether it's sharks or seagulls?"

"I won't do it!"

"Why don't we hear what the plan is first?" said the Old-Green-Grasshopper.

"I don't give a hoot what the plan is!" cried the Earthworm. "I am not going to be pecked to death by a bunch of seagulls!"

"You will be a martyr," said the Centipede. "I shall respect you for the rest of my life."

"So will I," said Miss Spider. "And your name will be in all the newspapers. Earthworm gives life to save friends . . ."

"But he won't *have* to give his life," James told them. "Now listen to me. This is what we'll do . . ."

21

"WHY, IT'S ABSOLUTELY BRILLIANT!" cried the Old-Green-Grasshopper when James had explained his plan.

"The boy's a genius!" the Centipede announced. "Now I can keep my boots on after all."

"Oh, I shall be pecked to death!" wailed the poor Earthworm.

"Of course you won't."

"I will, I know I will! And I won't even be able to see them coming at me because I have no eyes!"

James went over and put an arm gently around the Earthworm's shoulders. "I won't let them *touch* you," he said. "I promise I won't. But we've *got* to hurry! Look down there!"

There were more sharks than ever now around the peach. The water was boiling with them. There must have been ninety or a hundred at least. And to the travel-

ers up on top, it certainly seemed as though the peach were sinking lower and lower into the water.

"Action stations!" James shouted. "Jump to it! There's not a moment to lose!" He was the captain now, and everyone knew it. They would do whatever he told them.

"All hands below deck except Earthworm!" he ordered.

"Yes, yes!" they said eagerly as they scuttled into the tunnel entrance. "Come on! Let's hurry!"

"And you—Centipede!" James shouted. "Hop downstairs and get that Silkworm to work at once! Tell her to spin as she's never spun before! Our lives depend upon it! And the same applies to you, Miss Spider! Hurry on down! Start spinning!"

22

IN A FEW MINUTES everything was ready.

It was very quiet now on the top of the peach. There was nobody in sight—nobody except the Earthworm.

One half of the Earthworm, looking like a great, thick, juicy, pink sausage, lay innocently in the sun for all the seagulls to see.

The other half of him was dangling down the tunnel.

James was crouching close beside the Earthworm in the tunnel entrance, just below the surface, waiting for the first seagull. He had a loop of silk string in his hands.

The Old-Green-Grasshopper and the Ladybug were further down the tunnel, holding on to the Earthworm's tail, ready to pull him quickly in out of danger as soon as James gave the word.

And far below, in the great hollow stone of the peach, the Glow-worm was lighting up the room so that the two spinners, the Silkworm and Miss Spider, could see what they were doing. The Centipede was down there, too, exhorting them both frantically to greater efforts, and every now and again James could hear his voice coming up faintly from the depths, shouting, "Spin, Silkworm, spin, you great fat lazy brute! Faster, faster, or we'll throw you to the sharks!"

"Here comes the first seagull!" whispered James. "Keep still now, Earthworm. Keep still. The rest of you get ready to pull."

"Please don't let it spike me," begged the Earthworm.

"I won't, I won't. Ssshhh . . ."

Out of the corner of one eye, James watched the seagull as it came swooping down toward the Earthworm. And then suddenly it was so close that he could see its small black eyes and its curved beak, and the beak was open, ready to grab a nice piece of flesh out of the Earthworm's back.

"Pull!" shouted James.

The Old-Green-Grasshopper and the Ladybug gave the Earthworm's tail an enormous tug, and like magic the Earthworm disappeared into the tunnel. At the same time, up went James's hand and the seagull flew right into the loop of silk that he was holding out. The loop, which had been cleverly made, tightened just the right amount (but not too much) around its neck, and the seagull was captured.

"Hooray!" shouted the Old-Green-Grasshopper, peering out of the tunnel. "Well done, James!"

Up flew the seagull with James paying out the silk string as it went. He gave it about fifty yards and then tied the string to the stem of the peach.

"Next one!" he shouted, jumping back into the tunnel.

"Up you get again, Earthworm! Bring up some more silk, Centipede!"

"Oh, I don't like this at all," wailed the Earthworm. "It only just missed me! I even felt the wind on my back as it went swishing past!"

"Ssshh!" whispered James. "Keep still! Here comes another one!"

So they did it again.

And again, and again, and again.

And the seagulls kept coming, and James caught them one after the other and tethered them to the peach stem.

"One hundred seagulls!" he shouted, wiping the sweat from his face.

"Keep going!" they cried. "Keep going, James!"

"Two hundred seagulls!"

"Three hundred seagulls!"

"Four hundred seagulls!"

The sharks, as though sensing that they were in danger of losing their prey, were hurling themselves at the peach more furiously than ever, and the peach was sinking lower and lower still in the water.

"Five hundred seagulls!" James shouted.

"Silkworm says she's running out of silk!" yelled the Centipede from below. "She says she can't keep it up much longer. Nor can Miss Spider!"

"Tell them they've *got* to!" James answered. "They can't stop now!"

"We're lifting!" somebody shouted.

"No, we're not!"

"I felt it!"

"Put on another seagull, quick!"

"Quiet, everybody! Quiet! Here's one coming now!"

This was the five hundred and first seagull, and the moment that James caught it and tethered it to the stem with all the others, the whole enormous peach suddenly started rising up slowly out of the water.

"Look out! Here we go! Hold on, boys!"

But then it stopped.

And there it hung.

It hovered and swayed, but it went no higher.

The bottom of it was just touching the water. It was like a delicately balanced scale that needed only the tiniest push to tip it one way or the other.

"One more will do it!" shouted the Old-Green-Grasshopper, looking out of the tunnel. "We're almost there!"

And now came the big moment. Quickly, the five hundred and second seagull was caught and harnessed to the peach stem . . .

And then suddenly . . .

But slowly . . .

Majestically . . .

Like some fabulous golden balloon . . .

With all the seagulls straining at the strings above . . .

The giant peach rose up dripping out of the water and began climbing toward the heavens.

23

In a flash, everybody was up on top.

"Oh, isn't it beautiful!" they cried.

"What a marvelous feeling!"

"Good-by, sharks!"

"Oh, boy, this is the way to travel!"

Miss Spider, who was literally squealing with excitement, grabbed the Centipede by the waist and the two of them started dancing around and around the peach stem together. The Earthworm stood up on his tail and did a sort of wriggle of joy all by himself. The Old-Green-Grasshopper kept hopping higher and higher in the air. The Ladybug rushed over and shook James warmly by the hand. The Glow-worm, who at the best of times was a very shy and silent creature, sat glowing with pleasure near the tunnel entrance. Even the Silkworm, looking white and thin and completely exhausted, came creeping out of the tunnel to watch this miraculous ascent.

Up and up they went, and soon they were as high as the top of a church steeple above the ocean.

"I'm a bit worried about the peach," James said to the others as soon as all the dancing and the shouting had stopped. "I wonder how much damage those sharks have done to it underneath. It's quite impossible to tell from up here."

"Why don't I go over the side and make an inspection?" Miss Spider said. "It'll be no trouble at all, I assure you." And without waiting for an answer, she quickly produced a length of silk thread and attached the end of it to

the peach stem. "I'll be back in a jiffy," she said, and then she walked calmly over to the edge of the peach and jumped off, paying out the thread behind her as she fell.

The others crowded anxiously around the place where she had gone over.

"Wouldn't it be dreadful if the thread broke," the Ladybug said.

There was a rather long silence.

"Are you all right, Miss Spider?" shouted the Old-Green-Grasshopper.

"Yes, thank you!" her voice answered from below. "I'm coming up now!" And up she came, climbing foot over foot up the silk thread, and at the same time tucking the thread back cleverly into her body as she climbed past it.

"Is it *awful*?" they asked her. "Is it all eaten away? Are there great holes in it everywhere?"

Miss Spider clambered back onto the deck with a pleased but also rather puzzled look on her face. "You won't believe this," she said, "but actually there's hardly any damage down there at all! The peach is almost untouched! There are just a few tiny pieces out of it here and there, but nothing more."

"You must be mistaken," James told her.

"Of course she's mistaken!" the Centipede said.

"I promise you I'm not," Miss Spider answered.

"But there were hundreds of sharks around us!"

"They churned the water into a froth!"

"We saw their great mouths opening and shutting!"

"I don't care what you saw," Miss Spider answered. "They certainly didn't do much damage to the peach."

"Then why did we start sinking?" the Centipede asked.

"Perhaps we *didn't* start sinking," the Old-Green-Grasshopper suggested. "Perhaps we were all so frightened that we simply imagined it."

This, in point of fact, was closer to the truth than any of them knew. A shark, you see, has an extremely long sharp nose, and its mouth is set very awkwardly underneath its face and a long way back. This makes it more or less impossible for it to get its teeth into a vast smooth curving surface such as the side of a peach. Even if the creature turns onto its back it still can't do it, because the nose always gets in the way. If you have ever seen a small dog trying to get its teeth into an enormous ball, then you will be able to imagine roughly how it was with the sharks and the peach.

"It must have been some kind of magic," the Ladybug said. "The holes must have healed up by themselves."

"Oh, look! There's a ship below *us*!" shouted James.

Everybody rushed to the side and peered over. None of them had ever seen a ship before.

"It looks like a big one."

"It's got three funnels."

"You can even see the people on the decks!"

"Let's wave to them. Do you think they can see us?"

Neither James nor any of the others knew it, but the ship that was now passing beneath them was actually the Queen Mary sailing out of the English Channel on her way to America. And on the bridge of the Queen Mary, the astonished Captain was standing with a group of his officers, all of them gaping at the great round ball hovering overhead.

"I don't like it," the Captain said.

"Nor do I," said the First Officer.

"Do you think it's following us?" said the Second Officer.

"I tell you I don't like it," muttered the Captain.

"It could be dangerous," the First Officer said.

"That's it!" cried the Captain. "It's a secret weapon! Holy cats! Send a message to the Queen at once! The country must be warned! And give me my telescope."

The First Officer handed the telescope to the Captain. The Captain put it to his eye.

"There's birds everywhere!" he cried. "The whole sky is teeming with birds! What in the world are *they* doing? And wait! Wait a second! There are *people* on it! I can see them moving! There's a—a—do I have this darned thing focused right? It looks like a little boy in short trousers!

Yes, I can distinctly see a little boy in short trousers standing up there! And there's a—there's a—there's a—a—a—a sort of *giant ladybug*!"

"Now just a minute, Captain!" the First Officer said.

"And a *colossal green grasshopper*!"

"Captain!" the First Officer said sharply. "Captain, please!"

"And a *mammoth spider*!"

"Oh dear, he's been at the whisky again," whispered the Second Officer.

"And an *enormous—a simply enormous centipede*!" screamed the Captain.

"Call the Ship's Doctor," the First Officer said. "Our Captain is not well."

A moment later, the great round ball disappeared into a cloud, and the people on the ship never saw it again.

24

─────────

BUT UP ON the peach itself, everyone was still happy and excited.

"I wonder where we'll finish up this time," the Earthworm said.

"Who cares?" they answered. "Seagulls always go back to the land sooner or later."

Up and up they went, high above the highest clouds, the peach swaying gently from side to side as it floated along.

"Wouldn't this be a perfect time for a little music?" the ladybug asked. "How about it, Old Grasshopper?"

"With pleasure, dear lady," the Old-Green-Grasshopper answered, bowing from the waist.

"Oh, hooray! He's going to play for us!" they cried, and immediately the whole company sat themselves down in a circle around the Old Green Musician—and the concert began.

From the moment that the first note was struck, the audience became completely spellbound. And as for James, never had he heard such beautiful music as this! In the garden at home on summer evenings, he had listened many times to the sound of grasshoppers chirping in the grass, and he had always liked the noise that they made. But this was a different kind of noise altogether. This was real music—chords, harmonies, tunes, and all the rest of it.

And what a wonderful instrument the Old-Green-Grasshopper was playing on. It was like a violin! It was almost exactly as though he were playing upon a violin!

The bow of the violin, the part that moved, was his back leg. The strings of the violin, the part that made the sound, was the edge of his wing.

He was using only the top of his back leg (the thigh), and he was stroking this up and down against the edge of his wing with incredible skill, sometimes slowly, sometimes fast, but always with the same easy flowing action. It was precisely the way a clever violinist would have used his bow; and the music came pouring out and filled the whole blue sky around them with magic melodies.

When the first part was finished, everyone clapped madly, and Miss Spider stood up and shouted, "Bravo!

Encore! Give us some more!"

"Did you like that, James?" the Old-Green-Grasshopper asked, smiling at the small boy.

"Oh, I loved it!" James answered. "It was beautiful! It was as though you had a real violin in your hands!"

"A *real* violin!" the Old-Green-Grasshopper cried. "Good heavens, I like that! My dear boy, I *am* a real violin! It is part of my own body!"

"But do *all* grasshoppers play their music on violins, the same way as you do?" James asked him.

"No," he answered, "not all. If you want to know, I happen to be a 'short-horned' grasshopper. I have two short feelers coming out of my head. Can you see them? There they are. They are quite short, aren't they? That's why they call me a 'short-horn.' And we 'short-horns' are the only ones who play our music in the violin style, using a bow. My 'long-horned' relatives, the ones who have long curvy feelers coming out of their heads, make their music simply by rubbing the edges of their two top wings together. They are not violinists, they are wing-rubbers. And a rather inferior noise these wing-rubbers produce, too, if I may say so. It sounds more like a banjo than a fiddle."

"How fascinating this all is!" cried James. "And to think that up until now I had never even *wondered* how a grasshopper made his sounds."

"My dear young fellow," the Old-Green-Grasshopper said gently, "there are a whole lot of things in this world of ours that you haven't started wondering about yet. Where, for example, do you think that I keep my ears?"

"Your ears? Why, in your head, of course."

Everyone burst out laughing.

"You mean you don't even know *that*?" cried the Centipede.

"Try again," said the Old-Green-Grasshopper, smiling at James.

"You can't possibly keep them anywhere else?"

"Oh, can't I?"

"Well—I give up. Where *do* you keep them?"

"Right here," the Old-Green-Grasshopper said. "One on each side of my tummy."

"It's not true!"

"Of course it's true. What's so peculiar about that? You ought to see where my cousins the crickets and the katydids keep theirs."

"Where do they keep them?"

"In their legs. One in each front leg, just below the knee."

"You mean you didn't know that either?" the Centipede said scornfully.

"You're joking," James said. "Nobody could possibly have his ears in his legs."

"Why not?"

"Because . . . because it's ridiculous, that's why."

"You know what I think is ridiculous?" the Centipede said, grinning away as usual. "I don't mean to be rude, but *I* think it is ridiculous to have ears on the sides of one's head. It certainly *looks* ridiculous. You ought to take a peek in the mirror some day and see for yourself."

"Pest!" cried the Earthworm. "Why must you always be so rude and rambunctious to everyone? You ought to apologize to James at once."

25

JAMES DIDN'T WANT the Earthworm and the Centipede to get into another argument, so he said quickly to the Earthworm, "Tell me, do *you* play any kind of music?"

"No, but I do *other* things, some of which are really quite *extraordinary*," the Earthworm said, brightening.

"Such as what?" asked James.

"Well," the Earthworm said. "Next time you stand in a field or in a garden and look around you, then just remember this: that every grain of soil upon the surface of the land, every tiny little bit of soil that you can see, has actually passed through the body of an Earthworm during the last few years! Isn't that wonderful?"

"It's not possible!" said James.

"My dear boy, it's a fact."

"You mean you actually *swallow* soil?"

"Like mad," the Earthworm said proudly. "*In* one end and *out* the other."

"But what's the point?"

"What do you mean, what's the point?"

"Why do you do it?"

"We do it for the farmers. It makes the soil nice and light and crumbly so that things will grow well in it. If you really want to know, the farmers couldn't do without us. We are essential. We are vital. So it is only natural that the farmer should love us. He loves us even more, I believe, than he loves the Ladybug."

"The Ladybug!" said James, turning to look at her. "Do they love you, too?"

"I am told that they do," the Ladybug answered modestly, blushing all over. "In fact, I understand that in some places the farmers love us so much that they go out and buy live Ladybugs by the sackful and take them home and set them free in their fields. They are very pleased when they have lots of Ladybugs in their fields."

"But why?" James asked.

"Because we gobble up all the nasty little insects that are gobbling up all the farmer's crops. It helps enormously, and we ourselves don't charge a penny for our services."

"I think you're wonderful," James told her. "Can I ask you one special question?"

"Please do."

"Well, is it really true that I can tell how old a Ladybug is by counting her spots?"

"Oh no, that's just a children's story," the Ladybug said. "We never change our spots. Some of us, of course, are

born with more spots than others, but we never change them. The number of spots that a Ladybug has is simply a way of showing which branch of the family she belongs to. I, for example, as you can see for yourself, am a Nine-Spotted Ladybug. I am very lucky. It is a fine thing to be."

"It is, indeed," said James, gazing at the beautiful scarlet shell with the nine black spots on it.

"On the other hand," the Ladybug went on, "some of my less fortunate relatives have no more than two spots altogether on their shells! Can you imagine that? They are called Two-Spotted Ladybugs, and very common and ill-mannered they are, I regret to say. And then, of course, you have the Five-Spotted Ladybugs as well. They are much nicer than the Two-Spotted ones, although I myself find them a trifle too saucy for my taste."

"But they are all of them loved?" said James.

"Yes," the Ladybug answered quietly. "They are all of them loved."

"It seems that almost *everyone* around here is loved!" said James. "How nice this is!"

"Not me!" cried the Centipede happily. "I am a pest and I'm proud of it! Oh, I am such a shocking dreadful pest!"

"Hear, hear," the Earthworm said.

"But what about you, Miss Spider?" asked James. "Aren't you also much loved in the world?"

"Alas, no," Miss Spider answered, sighing long and loud. "I am not loved at all. And yet I do nothing but good. All day long I catch flies and mosquitoes in my webs. I am a decent person."

"I know you are," said James.

"It is very unfair the way we Spiders are treated," Miss Spider went on. "Why, only last week your own horrible Aunt Sponge flushed my poor dear father down the plughole in the bathtub."

"Oh, how awful!" cried James.

"I watched the whole thing from a corner up in the ceiling," Miss Spider murmured. "It was ghastly. We never saw him again." A large tear rolled down her cheek and fell with a splash on the floor.

"But is it not very unlucky to kill a spider?" James inquired, looking around at the others.

"Of course it's unlucky to kill a spider!" shouted the Centipede. "It's about the unluckiest thing anyone can do. Look what happened to Aunt Sponge after she'd done that! *Bump!* We all felt it, didn't we, as the peach went over her? Oh, what a lovely bump that must have been for you, Miss Spider!"

"It was very satisfactory," Miss Spider answered. "Will you sing us a song about it, please?"

So the Centipede did.

"Aunt Sponge was terrifically fat,
And tremendously flabby at that.
Her tummy and waist
Were as soggy as paste—
It was worse on the place where she sat!

So she said, 'I must make myself flat.
I must make myself sleek as a cat.
I shall do without dinner
To make myself thinner.'
But along came the peach!
Oh, the beautiful peach!
And made her far thinner than that!"

"That was very nice," Miss Spider said. "Now sing one about Aunt Spiker."

"With pleasure," the Centipede answered, grinning:

"Aunt Spiker was thin as a wire,
And as dry as a bone, only drier.
She was so long and thin
If you carried her in
You could use her for poking the fire!

'I must do something quickly,' she frowned.
'I want FAT. *I want pound upon pound!*
I must eat lots and lots
Of marshmallows and chocs
Till I start bulging out all around.'

'Ah, yes,' she announced, 'I have sworn
That I'll alter my figure by dawn!'
Cried the peach with a snigger,
'I'LL alter your figure—'
And ironed her out on the lawn!"

Everybody clapped and called out for more songs from the Centipede, who at once launched into his favorite song of all:

"Once upon a time
When pigs were swine
And monkeys chewed tobacco
And hens took snuff
To make themselves tough
And the ducks said quack-quack-quacko,
And porcupines
Drank fiery wines
And goats ate tapioca
And Old Mother Hubbard
Got stuck in the c—"

"Look out, Centipede!" cried James. "Look out!"

26

THE CENTIPEDE, who had begun dancing wildly around the deck during the song, had suddenly gone too close to the downward curving edge of the peach, and for three awful seconds he had stood teetering on the brink, swinging his legs frantically in circles in an effort to stop himself from falling over backward into space. But before anyone could reach him—down he went! He gave a shriek of terror as he fell, and the others, rushing to the side and peering over, saw his poor long body tumbling over and over through the air, getting smaller and smaller until it was out of sight.

"Silkworm!" yelled James. "Quick! Start spinning!"

The Silkworm sighed, for she was still very tired from spinning all that silk for the seagulls, but she did as she was told.

"I'm going down after him!" cried James, grabbing the silk string as it started coming out of the Silkworm and tying the end of it around his waist. "The rest of you hold on to Silkworm so I don't pull her over with me, and later on, if you feel three tugs on the string, start hauling me up again!"

He jumped, and he went tumbling down after the Centipede, down, down, down, toward the sea below, and you can imagine how quickly the Silkworm had to spin to keep up with the speed of his fall.

"We'll never see either of them again!" cried the Ladybug. "Oh, dear! Oh, dear! Just when we were all so happy, too!"

Miss Spider, the Glow-worm, and the Ladybug all began to cry. So did the Earthworm. "I don't care a bit about the Centipede," the Earthworm sobbed. "But I really did love that little boy."

Very softly, the Old-Green-Grasshopper started to play the Funeral March on his violin, and by the time he had finished, everyone, including himself, was in a flood of tears.

Suddenly, there came three sharp tugs on the rope. "Pull!" shouted the Old-Green-Grasshopper. "Everyone get behind me and pull!"

There was about a mile of string to be hauled in, but they all worked like mad, and in the end, over the side of the peach, there appeared a dripping-wet James with a dripping-wet Centipede clinging to him tightly with all forty-two of his legs.

"He saved me!" gasped the Centipede. "He swam around in the middle of the Atlantic Ocean until he found me!"

"My dear boy," the Old-Green-Grasshopper said, patting James on the back. "I do congratulate you."

"My boots!" cried the Centipede. "Just look at my precious boots! They are ruined by the water!"

"Be quiet!" the Earthworm said. "You are lucky to be alive."

"Are we still going up and up?" asked James.

"We certainly are," answered the Old-Green-Grasshopper. "And it's beginning to get dark."

"I know. It'll soon be night."

"Why don't we all go down below and keep warm until tomorrow morning?" Miss Spider suggested.

"No," the Old-Green-Grasshopper said. "I think that would be very unwise. It will be safer if we all stay up here through the night and keep watch. Then, if anything happens, we shall anyway be ready for it."

27

JAMES HENRY TROTTER and his companions crouched close together on top of the peach as the night began closing in around them. Clouds like mountains towered high above their heads on all sides, mysterious, menacing, overwhelming. Gradually it grew darker and darker, and then a pale three-quarter moon came up over the tops of the clouds and cast an eerie light over the whole scene. The giant peach swayed gently from side to side as it floated along, and the hundreds of silky white strings going upward from its stem were beautiful in the moonlight. So also was the great flock of seagulls overhead.

There was not a sound anywhere. Traveling upon the peach was not in the least like traveling in an airplane.

The airplane comes clattering and roaring through the sky, and whatever might be lurking secretly up there in the great cloud-mountains goes running for cover at its approach. That is why people who travel in airplanes never see anything.

But the peach . . . ah, yes . . . the peach was a soft, stealthy traveler, making no noise at all as it floated along. And several times during that long silent night ride high up over the middle of the ocean in the moonlight, James and his friends saw things that no one had ever seen before.

Once, as they drifted silently past a massive white cloud, they saw on the top of it a group of strange, tall, wispy-looking things that were about twice the height of ordinary men. They were not easy to see at first because they were almost as white as the cloud itself, but as the

peach sailed closer, it became obvious that these "things" were actually living creatures—tall, wispy, wraithlike, shadowy white creatures who looked as though they were made out of a mixture of cotton-wool and candy-floss and thin white hairs.

"Ooooooooooooooh!" the Ladybug said. "I don't like this at all!"

"Ssshh!" James whispered back. "Don't let them hear you! They must be Cloud-Men!"

"Cloud-Men!" they murmured, huddling closer together for comfort. "Oh dear, oh dear!"

"I'm glad I'm blind and can't see them," the Earthworm said, "or I would probably scream."

"I hope they don't turn around and see *us*," Miss Spider stammered.

"Do you think they would eat us?" the Earthworm asked.

"They would eat *you*," the Centipede answered, grinning. "They would cut you up like a salami and eat you in thin slices."

The poor Earthworm began to quiver all over with fright.

"But what are they *doing*?" the Old-Green-Grasshopper whispered.

"I don't know," James answered softly. "Let's watch and see."

The Cloud-Men were all standing in a group, and they were doing something peculiar with their hands. First, they would reach out (all of them at once) and grab handfuls of cloud. Then they would roll these handfuls of cloud in their fingers until they turned into what looked like large white marbles. Then they would toss the marbles to one side and quickly grab more bits of cloud and start over again.

It was all very silent and mysterious. The pile of marbles beside them kept growing larger and larger. Soon there was a truckload of them there at least.

"They must be absolutely mad!" the Centipede said. "There's nothing to be afraid of here!"

"Be quiet, you pest!" the Earthworm whispered. "We shall all be eaten if they see us!"

But the Cloud-Men were much too busy with what they were doing to have noticed the great peach floating silently up behind them.

Then the watchers on the peach saw one of the Cloud-Men raising his long wispy arms above his head and they heard him shouting, "All right, boys! That's enough! Get the shovels!" And all the other Cloud-Men immediately let out a strange high-pitched whoop of joy and started jumping up and down and waving their arms in the air. Then they picked up enormous shovels and rushed over to the pile of marbles and began shoveling them as fast as they could over the side of the cloud, into space. *"Down they go!"* they chanted as they worked.

"Down they go!
Hail and snow!
Freezes and sneezes and noses will blow!"

"It's *hailstones*!" whispered James excitedly. "They've been making hailstones and now they are showering them down onto the people in the world below!"

"Hailstones?" the Centipede said. "That's ridiculous!

This is summertime. You don't have hailstones in summertime."

"They are practicing for the winter," James told him.

"I don't believe it!" shouted the Centipede, raising his voice.

"Ssshh!" the others whispered. And James said softly, "For heaven's sake, Centipede, don't make so much noise."

The Centipede roared with laughter. "Those imbeciles couldn't hear anything!" he cried. "They're deaf as door-knobs! You watch!" And before anyone could stop him, he had cupped his front feet to his mouth and was yelling at the Cloud-Men as loud as he could. "Idiots!" he yelled. "Nincompoops! Half-wits! Blunderheads! Asses! What on earth do you think you're doing over there!"

The effect was immediate. The Cloud-Men jumped around as if they had been stung by wasps. And when they saw the great golden peach floating past them not fifty yards away in the sky, they gave a yelp of surprise and dropped their shovels to the ground. And there they stood with the moonlight streaming down all over them, absolutely motionless, like a group of tall white hairy statues, staring and staring at the gigantic fruit as it went sailing by.

The passengers on the peach (all except the Centipede) sat frozen with terror, looking back at the Cloud-Men and wondering what was going to happen next.

"Now you've done it, you loathsome pest!" whispered the Earthworm to the Centipede.

"I'm not frightened of *them*!" shouted the Centipede, and to show everybody once again that he wasn't, he stood up to his full height and started dancing about and making insulting signs at the Cloud-Men with all forty-two of his legs.

This evidently infuriated the Cloud-Men beyond belief. All at once, they spun around and grabbed great handfuls of hailstones and rushed to the edge of the cloud and started throwing them at the peach, shrieking with fury all the time.

"Look out!" cried James. "Quick! Lie down! Lie flat on the deck!"

It was lucky they did! A large hailstone can hurt you as much as a rock or a lump of lead if it is thrown hard enough—and my goodness, how those Cloud-Men could throw! The hailstones came whizzing through the air like bullets from a machine gun, and James could hear them smashing against the sides of the peach and burying themselves in the peach flesh with horrible squelching noises—*plop! plop! plop! plop!* And then *ping! ping! ping!* as they bounced off the poor Ladybug's shell because she couldn't lie as flat as the others. And then *crack!* as one of them hit the Centipede right on the nose and *crack!* again as another one hit him somewhere else.

"Ow!" he cried. "Ow! Stop! Stop! Stop!"

But the Cloud-Men had no intention of stopping. James could see them rushing about on the cloud like a lot of huge hairy ghosts, picking up hailstones from the pile, dashing to the edge of the cloud, hurling the hailstones at the peach, dashing back again to get more, and then, when the pile of stones was all gone, they simply grabbed handfuls of cloud and made as many more as they wanted, and much bigger ones now, some of them as large as cannon balls.

"Quickly!" cried James. "Down the tunnel or we'll all be wiped out!"

There was a rush for the tunnel entrance, and half a minute later everybody was safely downstairs inside the stone of the peach, trembling with fright and listening to the noise of the hailstones as they came crashing against the side of the peach.

"I'm a wreck!" groaned the Centipede. "I am wounded all over!"

"It serves you right," said the Earthworm.

"Would somebody kindly look and see if my shell is cracked?" the Ladybug said.

"Give us some light!" shouted the Old-Green-Grass-hopper.

"I can't!" wailed the Glow-worm. "They've broken my bulb!"

"Then put in another one!" the Centipede said.

"Be quiet a moment," said James. "Listen! I do believe they're not hitting us any more!"

They all stopped talking and listened. Yes—the noise had ceased! The hailstones were no longer smashing against the peach.

"We've left them behind!"

"The seagulls must have pulled us away out of danger!"

"Hooray! Let's go up and see!"

Cautiously, with James going first, they all climbed back up the tunnel. James poked his head out and looked around. "It's all clear!" he called. "I can't see them any-where!"

28

One by one, the travelers came out again onto the top of the peach and gazed carefully around. The moon was still shining as brightly as ever, and there were still plenty of huge shimmering cloud-mountains on all sides. But there were no Cloud-Men in sight now.

"The peach is leaking!" shouted the Old-Green-Grasshopper, peering over the side. "It's full of holes and the juice is dripping out everywhere!"

"*That* does it!" cried the Earthworm. "If the peach is leaking then we shall surely sink!"

"Don't be an ass!" the Centipede told him. "We're not in the water now!"

"Oh, look!" shouted the Ladybug. "Look, look, look! Over there!"

Everybody swung round to look.

In the distance and directly ahead of them, they now saw a most extraordinary sight. It was a kind of arch, a colossal curvy-shaped thing that reached high up into the sky and came down again at both ends. The ends were resting upon a huge flat cloud that was as big as a desert.

"Now what in the world is that?" asked James.

"It's a bridge!"

"It's an enormous hoop cut in half!"

"It's a giant horseshoe standing upside down!"

"Stop me if I'm wrong," murmured the Centipede, going white in the face, "but might those not be Cloud-Men climbing all over it?"

There was a dreadful silence. The peach floated closer and closer.

"They *are* Cloud-Men!"

"There are hundreds of them!"

"Thousands!"

"Millions!"

"I don't want to hear about it!" shrieked the poor blind Earthworm. "I'd rather be on the end of a fish hook and used as bait than come up against those terrible creatures again!"

"I'd rather be fried alive and eaten by a Mexican!" wailed the Old-Green-Grasshopper.

"Please keep quiet," whispered James. "It's our only hope."

They crouched very still on top of the peach, staring at the Cloud-Men. The whole surface of the cloud was literally *swarming* with them, and there were hundreds more up above, climbing about on that monstrous crazy arch.

"But what *is* that thing?" whispered the Ladybug. "And what are they *doing* to it?"

"I don't care what they're doing to it!" the Centipede said, scuttling over to the tunnel entrance. "I'm not staying up here! Good-by!"

But the rest of them were too frightened or too hypnotized by the whole affair to make a move.

"Do you know what?" James whispered.

"What?" they said. *"What?"*

"That enormous arch—they seem to be *painting* it! They've got pots of paint and big brushes! You look!"

And he was quite right. The travelers were close

enough now to see that this was exactly what the Cloud-Men were doing. They all had huge brushes in their hands and they were splashing the paint onto the great curvy arch in a frenzy of speed, so fast, in fact, that in a few minutes the whole of the arch became covered with the most glorious colors—reds, blues, greens, yellows, and purples.

"It's a rainbow!" everyone said at once. "They are making a rainbow!"

"Oh, isn't it beautiful!"

"Just look at those colors!"

"Centipede!" they shouted. "You *must* come up and see this!" They were so enthralled by the beauty and brilliance of the rainbow that they forgot to keep their voices low any longer. The Centipede poked his head cautiously out of the tunnel entrance.

"Well well well," he said. "I've *always* wondered how those things were made. But why all the ropes? What are they doing with those ropes?"

"Good heavens, they are pushing it off the cloud!" cried James. "There it goes! They are lowering it down to the earth with ropes!"

"And I'll tell you something else," the Centipede said sharply. "If I'm not greatly mistaken, we ourselves are going to bump right into it!"

"Bless my soul, he's right!" the Old-Green-Grasshopper exclaimed.

The rainbow was now dangling in the air below the cloud. The peach was also just below the level of the cloud, and it was heading directly toward the rainbow, traveling rather fast.

"We are lost!" Miss Spider cried, wringing her feet again. "The end has come!"

"I can't stand it!" wailed the Earthworm. "Tell me what's happening!"

"We're going to miss it!" shouted the Ladybug.

"No, we're not!"

"Yes, we are!"

"Yes!—Yes!—No!—Oh, my heavens!"

"Hold on, everybody!" James called out, and suddenly

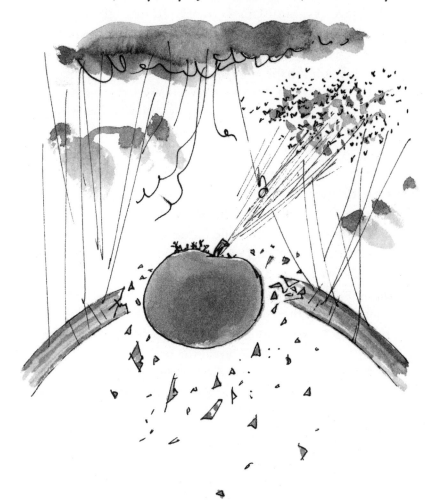

there was a tremendous thud as the peach went crashing into the top part of the rainbow. This was followed by an awful splintering noise as the enormous rainbow snapped right across the middle and became two separate pieces.

The next thing that happened was extremely unfortunate. The ropes that the Cloud-Men had been using for lowering the rainbow got tangled up with the silk strings that went up from the peach to the seagulls! The peach was trapped! Panic and pandemonium broke out among the travelers, and James Henry Trotter, glancing up quickly, saw the faces of a thousand furious Cloud-Men peering down at him over the edge of the cloud. The faces had almost no shape at all because of the long white hairs that covered them. There were no noses, no mouths, no ears, no chins—only the eyes were visible in each face, two small black eyes glinting malevolently through the hairs.

Then came the most frightening thing of all. One Cloud-Man, a huge hairy creature who must have been fourteen feet tall at least, suddenly stood up and made a tremendous leap off the side of the cloud, trying to get to one of the silk strings above the peach. James and his friends saw him go flying through the air above them, his arms outstretched in front of him, reaching for the nearest string, and they saw him grab it and cling to it with his hands and legs. And then, very very slowly, hand over hand, he began to come down the string.

"Mercy! Help! Save us!" cried the Ladybug.

"He's coming down to eat us!" wailed the Old-Green-Grasshopper. "Jump overboard!"

"Then eat the Earthworm first!" shouted the Cen-

tipede. "It's no good eating me, I'm full of bones like a kipper!"

"Centipede!" yelled James. "Quickly! Bite through that string, the one he's coming down on!"

The Centipede rushed over to the stem of the peach and took the silk string in his teeth and bit through it with one snap of his jaws. Immediately, far above them, a single seagull was seen to come away from the rest of the flock and go flying off with a long string trailing from its neck. And clinging desperately to the end of the string, shouting and cursing with fury, was the huge hairy Cloud-Man. Up and up he went, swinging across the moonlit sky, and James Henry Trotter, watching him with delight, said, "My goodness, he must weigh almost nothing at all for one seagull to be able to pull him up like that! He must be all hair and air!"

The rest of the Cloud-Men were so flabbergasted at seeing one of their company carried away in this manner that they let go the ropes they were holding, and then of course down went the rainbow, both halves of it together, tumbling toward the earth below. This freed the peach, which at once began sailing away from that terrible cloud.

But the travelers were not in the clear yet. The infuriated Cloud-Men jumped up and ran after them along the cloud, pelting them mercilessly with all sorts of hard and horrible objects. Empty paint buckets, paint brushes, stepladders, stools, saucepans, frying-pans, rotten eggs, dead rats, bottles of hair-oil—anything those brutes could lay their hands on came raining down upon the peach. One Cloud-Man, taking very careful aim, tipped a gallon of thick purple paint over the edge of the cloud right onto the Centipede himself.

The Centipede screamed with anger. "My legs!" he cried. "They are all sticking together! I can't walk! And my eyelids won't open! I can't see! And my boots! My boots are ruined!"

But for the moment everyone was far too busy dodging the things that the Cloud-Men were throwing to pay any attention to the Centipede.

"The paint is drying!" he moaned. "It's going hard! I

can't move my legs! I can't move anything!"

"You can still move your mouth," the Earthworm said. "And that is a great pity."

"James!" bawled the Centipede. "Please help me! Wash off this paint! Scrape it off! Anything!"

29

It seemed like a long time before the seagulls were able to pull the peach away from that horrible rainbow-cloud. But they managed it at last, and then everybody gathered around the wretched Centipede and began arguing about the best way to get the paint off his body.

He really did look a sight. He was purple all over, and now that the paint was beginning to dry and harden, he was forced to sit very stiff and upright, as though he were encased in cement. And all forty-two of his legs were sticking out straight in front of him, like rods. He tried to say something, but his lips wouldn't move. All he could do now was to make gurgling noises in his throat.

The Old-Green-Grasshopper reached out and touched him carefully on the stomach. "But how could it possibly have dried so quickly?" he asked.

"It's rainbow-paint," James answered. "Rainbow-paint dries very quick and very hard."

"I detest paint," Miss Spider announced. "It frightens me. It reminds me of Aunt Spiker—the *late* Aunt Spiker, I mean—because the last time she painted her kitchen

ceiling my poor darling grandmother stepped into it by
mistake when it was still wet, and there she stuck. And all
through the night we could hear her calling to us, saying
'Help! help! help!' and it was heartbreaking to listen to
her. But what could we do? Not a thing until the next day
when the paint had dried, and then of course we all
rushed over to her and calmed her down and gave her
some food. Believe it or not, she lived for six months like
that, upside down on the ceiling with her legs stuck permanently in the paint. She really did. We fed her every
day. We brought her fresh flies straight from the web. But
then on the twenty-sixth of April last, Aunt Sponge—the
late Aunt Sponge, I mean—happened to glance up at the
ceiling, and she spotted her. 'A spider!' she cried. 'A disgusting spider! Quick! Fetch me the mop with the long

handle!' And then—Oh, it was so awful I can't bear to think of it. . . ." Miss Spider wiped away a tear and looked sadly at the Centipede. "You poor thing," she murmured. "I do feel sorry for you."

"It'll never come off," the Earthworm said brightly. "Our Centipede will never move again. He will turn into a statue and we shall be able to put him in the middle of the lawn with a bird-bath on the top of his head."

"We could try peeling him like a banana," the Old-Green-Grasshopper suggested.

"Or rubbing him with sandpaper," the Ladybug said.

"Now if he stuck out his tongue," the Earthworm said, smiling a little for perhaps the first time in his life, "if he stuck it out really far, then we could all catch hold of it and start pulling. And if we pulled hard enough we could turn him inside out and he would have a new skin!"

There was a pause while the others considered this interesting proposal.

"I think," James said slowly, "I think that the best thing to do . . ." Then he stopped. "What was *that*?" he asked quickly. "I heard a voice! I heard someone shouting!"

30

THEY ALL RAISED their heads, listening.

"Ssshh! There it is again!"

But the voice was too far away for them to hear what it was saying.

"It's a Cloud-Man!" Miss Spider cried. "I just know it's a Cloud-Man! They're after us again!"

"It came from above!" the Earthworm said, and automatically everybody looked upward, everybody except the Centipede, who couldn't move.

"Ouch!" they said. "Help! Mercy! We're going to catch it this time!" For what they now saw, swirling and twisting directly over their heads, was an immense black cloud, a terrible, dangerous, thundery-looking thing that began to rumble and roar even as they were staring at it. And then, from high up on the top of the cloud, the faraway voice came down to them once again, this time very loud and clear.

"On with the faucets!" it shouted. *"On with the faucets! On with the faucets!"*

Three seconds later, the whole underneath of the cloud seemed to split and burst open like a paper bag, and then—*out* came the water! They saw it coming. It was quite easy to see because it wasn't just raindrops. It wasn't raindrops at all. It was a great solid mass of water that might have been a lake or a whole ocean dropping out of the sky on top of them, and down it came, down and down and down, crashing first onto the seagulls and then onto the peach itself, while the poor travelers shrieked with fear and groped around frantically for something to catch hold of—the peach stem, the silk strings, anything they could find—and all the time the water came pouring and roaring down upon them, bouncing and smashing and sloshing and slashing and swashing and swirling and surging and whirling and gurgling and gushing and rushing and rushing, and it was like

being pinned down underneath the biggest waterfall in the world and not being able to get out. They couldn't speak. They couldn't see. They couldn't breathe. And James Henry Trotter, holding on madly to one of the silk strings above the peach stem, told himself that this must surely be the end of everything at last. But then, just as suddenly as it had started, the deluge stopped. They were out of it and it was all over. The wonderful seagulls had flown right through it and had come out safely on the other side. Once again the giant peach was sailing peacefully through the mysterious moonlit sky.

"I am drowned!" gasped the Old-Green-Grasshopper, spitting out water by the pint.

"It's gone right through my skin!" the Earthworm groaned. "I always thought my skin was waterproof but it isn't and now I'm full of rain!"

"Look at me, look at me!" shouted the Centipede excitedly. "It's washed me *clean*! The paint's all gone! I can move again!"

"That's the worst news I've had in a long time," the Earthworm said.

The Centipede was dancing around the deck and turning somersaults in the air and singing at the top of his voice:

> *"Oh, hooray for the storm and the rain!*
> *I can move! I don't feel any pain!*

And now I'm a pest,
I'm the biggest and best,
The most marvelous pest once again!"

"Oh, do shut up," the Old-Green-Grasshopper said.
"Look at me!" cried the Centipede.

"Look at ME! I am freed! I am freed!
Not a scratch nor a bruise nor a bleed!
To his grave this fine gent
They all thought they had sent
And I very near went!
Oh, I VERY near went!
But they cent quite the wrong Sentipede!"

31

"HOW FAST WE ARE GOING all of a sudden," the Ladybug
said. "I wonder why?"

"I don't think the seagulls like this place any better
than we do," James answered. "I imagine they want to get
out of it as soon as they can. They got a bad fright in the
storm we've just been through."

Faster and faster flew the seagulls, skimming across
the sky at a tremendous pace, with the peach trailing out
behind them. Cloud after cloud went by on either side, all
of them ghostly white in the moonlight, and several more
times during the night the travelers caught glimpses of

Cloud-Men moving around on the tops of these clouds, working their sinister magic upon the world below.

Once they passed a snow machine in operation, with the Cloud-Men turning the handle and a blizzard of snow-flakes blowing out of the great funnel above. They saw the huge drums that were used for making thunder, and the Cloud-Men beating them furiously with long hammers. They saw the frost factories and the wind producers and the places where cyclones and tornadoes were manufactured and sent spinning down toward the Earth, and once, deep in the hollow of a large billowy cloud, they spotted something that could only have been a Cloud-Men's city. There were caves everywhere running into the cloud, and at the entrances to the caves the Cloud-Men's wives were crouching over little stoves with frying-pans in their hands, frying snowballs for their husbands' suppers. And hundreds of Cloud-Men's children were frisking about all over the place and shrieking with laughter and sliding down the billows of the cloud on toboggans.

An hour later, just before dawn, the travelers heard a soft *whooshing* noise above their heads and they glanced up and saw an immense gray batlike creature swooping down toward them out of the dark. It circled round and round the peach, flapping its great wings slowly in the moonlight and staring at the travelers. Then it uttered a series of long deep melancholy cries and flew off again into the night.

"Oh, I do wish the morning would come!" Miss Spider said, shivering all over.

"It won't be long now," James answered. "Look, it's getting lighter over there already."

They all sat in silence watching the sun as it came up slowly over the rim of the horizon for a new day.

32

AND WHEN FULL DAYLIGHT came at last, they all got to their feet and stretched their poor cramped bodies, and then the Centipede, who always seemed to see things first, shouted, "Look! There's land below!"

"He's right!" they cried, running to the edge of the peach and peering over. "Hooray! Hooray!"

"It looks like streets and houses!"

"But how enormous it all is!"

A vast city, glistening in the early-morning sunshine, lay spread out three thousand feet below them. At that height, the cars were like little beetles crawling along the streets, and people walking on the pavements looked no larger than tiny grains of soot.

"But what tremendous tall buildings!" exclaimed the Ladybug. "I've never seen anything like *them* before in England. Which town do you think it is?"

"This couldn't possibly be England," said the Old-Green-Grasshopper.

"Then where is it?" asked Miss Spider.

"You know what those buildings are?" shouted James, jumping up and down with excitement. "Those are sky-scrapers! So this must be America! And that, my friends, means that we have crossed the Atlantic Ocean over-night!"

"You don't mean it!" they cried.

"It's not possible!"

"It's incredible! It's unbelievable!"

"Oh, I've always dreamed of going to America!" cried the Centipede. "I had a friend once who—"

"Be quiet!" said the Earthworm. "Who cares about your friend? The thing we've got to think about now is *how on earth are we going to get down to earth?*"

"Ask James," said the Ladybug.

"I don't think that should be so very difficult," James told them. "All we'll have to do is to cut loose a few seagulls. Not too many, mind you, but just enough so that the others can't *quite* keep us up in the air. Then down we shall go, slowly and gently, until we reach the ground. Centipede will bite through the strings for us one at a time."

33

Far below them, in the City of New York, something like pandemonium was breaking out. A great round ball as big as a house had been sighted hovering high up in the sky over the very center of Manhattan, and the cry had gone up that it was an enormous bomb sent over by another country to blow the whole city to smithereens. Air-raid sirens began wailing in every section. All radio and television programs were interrupted with announcements that the population must go down into their cellars immediately. One million people walking in the streets on their way to work looked up into the sky and saw the monster hovering above them, and started running for the nearest subway entrance to take cover. Generals grabbed hold of telephones and shouted orders to everyone they could think of. The Mayor of New York called up the President of the United States down in Washington, D.C., to ask him for help, and the President, who at that moment was having breakfast in his pajamas, quickly pushed away his half-finished plate of Sugar Crisps and started pressing buttons right and left to summon his

Admirals and his Generals. And all the way across the vast stretch of America, in all the fifty States from Alaska to Florida, from Pennsylvania to Hawaii, the alarm was sounded and the word went out that the biggest bomb in the history of the world was hovering over New York City, and that at any moment it might go off.

34

"COME ON, CENTIPEDE, bite through the first string," James ordered.

The Centipede took one of the silk strings between his teeth and bit through it. And once again (but *not* with an angry Cloud-Man dangling from the end of the string this time) a single seagull came away from the rest of the flock and went flying off on its own.

"Bite another," James ordered.

The Centipede bit through another string.

"Why aren't we sinking?"

"We are sinking!"

"No, we're not!"

"Don't forget the peach is a lot lighter now than when we started out," James told them. "It lost an awful lot of juice when all those hailstones hit it in the night. Cut away two more seagulls, Centipede!"

"Ah, that's better!"

"Here we go!"

"Now we really are sinking!"

"Yes, this is perfect! Don't bite any more, Centipede, or we'll sink too fast! Gently does it!"

Slowly the great peach began losing height, and the buildings and streets down below began coming closer and closer.

"Do you think we'll all get our pictures in the papers when we get down?" the Ladybug asked.

"My goodness, I've forgotten to polish my boots!" the Centipede said. "Everyone must help me to polish my boots before we arrive."

"Oh, for heaven's sake!" said the Earthworm. "Can't you ever stop thinking about—"

But he never finished his sentence. For suddenly . . . *WHOOOSH!* . . . and they looked up and saw a huge four-engined plane come shooting out of a nearby cloud and go whizzing past them not more than twenty feet over their heads. This was actually the regular early-morning passenger plane coming in to New York from Chicago, and as it went by, it sliced right through every single one of the silken strings, and immediately the seagulls broke away, and the enormous peach, having nothing to hold it up in the air any longer, went tumbling down toward the earth like a lump of lead.

"Help!" cried the Centipede.

"Save us!" cried Miss Spider.

"We are lost!" cried the Ladybug.

"This is the end!" cried the Old-Green-Grasshopper.

"James!" cried the Earthworm. "Do something, James! Quickly, do something!"

"I can't!" cried James. "I'm sorry! Good-by! Shut your eyes, everybody! It won't be long now!"

35

ROUND AND ROUND and upside down went the peach as it plummeted toward the earth, and they were all clinging desperately to the stem to save themselves from being flung into space.

Faster and faster it fell. Down and down and down, racing closer and closer to the houses and streets below, where it would surely smash into a million pieces when it hit. And all the way along Fifth Avenue and Madison Avenue, and along all the other streets in the City, people who had not yet reached the underground shelters looked up and saw it coming, and they stopped running and stood there staring in a sort of stupor at what they thought was the biggest bomb in all the world falling out of the sky onto their heads. A few women screamed. Others knelt down on the sidewalks and began praying aloud. Strong men turned to one another and said things like, "I guess this is it, Joe," and "Good-by, everybody, good-by." And for the next thirty seconds the whole City held its breath, waiting for the end to come.

36

"GOOD-BY, LADYBUG!" gasped James, clinging to the stem of the falling peach. "Good-by, Centipede. Good-by, everybody!" There were only a few seconds to go now and it looked as though they were going to fall right in among all the tallest buildings. James could see the skyscrapers rushing up to meet them at the most awful speed, and most of them had square flat tops, but the very tallest of them all had a top that tapered off into a long sharp point—like an enormous silver needle sticking up into the sky.

And it was precisely onto the top of this needle that the peach fell!

There was a squelch. The needle went in deep. And suddenly—there was the giant peach, caught and spiked upon the very pinnacle of the Empire State Building.

37

IT WAS REALLY an amazing sight, and in two or three minutes, as soon as the people below realized that this now couldn't possibly be a bomb, they came pouring out of the shelters and the subways to gape at the marvel. The streets for half a mile around the building were jammed with men and women, and when the word spread that there were actually living things moving about on the top of the great round ball, then everyone went wild with excitement.

"It's a flying saucer!" they shouted.

"They are from Outer Space!"

"They are men from Mars!"

"Or maybe they came from the Moon!"

And a man who had a pair of binoculars to his eyes said, "They look *pritt*-ty peculiar to me, I'll tell you that."

Police cars and fire engines came screaming in from all over the city and pulled up outside the Empire State Building. Two hundred firemen and six hundred policemen swarmed into the building and went up in the elevators as high as they could go. Then they poured out onto the observation roof—which is the place where tourists stand—just at the bottom of the big spike.

All the policemen were holding their guns at the ready, with their fingers on the triggers, and the firemen were clutching their hatchets. But from where they stood, almost directly underneath the peach, they couldn't actually see the travelers up on top.

"Ahoy there!" shouted the Chief of Police. "Come out and show yourselves!"

Suddenly, the great brown head of the Centipede appeared over the side of the peach. His black eyes, as large and round as two marbles, glared down at the policemen and the firemen below. Then his monstrous ugly face broke into a wide grin.

The policemen and the firemen all started shouting at once. "Look out!" they cried. "It's a Dragon!"

"It's not a Dragon! It's a Wampus!"

"It's a Gorgon!"

"It's a Sea-serpent!"

"It's a Prock!"

"It's a Manticore!"

Three firemen and five policemen fainted and had to be carried away.

"It's a Snozzwanger!" cried the Chief of Police.

"It's a Whangdoodle!" yelled the Head of the Fire Department.

The Centipede kept on grinning. He seemed to be enjoying enormously the commotion that he was causing.

"Now see here!" shouted the Chief of Police, cupping his hands to his mouth. "You listen to me! I want you to tell me exactly where you've come from!"

"We've come from thousands of miles away!" the Centipede shouted back, grinning more broadly than ever and showing his brown teeth.

"There you are!" cried the Chief of Police. "I *told* you they came from Mars!"

"I guess you're right!" said the Head of the Fire Department.

At this point, the Old-Green-Grasshopper poked his huge green head over the side of the peach, alongside the Centipede's. Six more big strong men fainted when they saw him.

"That one's an Oinck!" screamed the Head of the Fire Department. "I just *know* it's an Oinck!"

"Or a Cockatrice!" yelled the Chief of Police. "Stand back, men! It may jump down on us any moment!"

"What on earth are they talking about?" the Old-Green-Grasshopper said to the Centipede.

"Search me," the Centipede answered. "But they seem to be in an awful stew about something."

Then Miss Spider's large black murderous-looking head, which to a stranger was probably the most terrifying of all, appeared next to the Grasshopper's.

"Snakes and ladders!" yelled the Head of the Fire Department. "We are finished now! It's a giant Scorpula!"

"It's worse than that!" cried the Chief of Police. "It's a vermicious Knid! Oh, just look at its vermicious gruesome face!"

"Is that the kind that eats fully grown men for breakfast?" the Head of the Fire Department asked, going white as a sheet.

"I'm afraid it is," the Chief of Police answered.

"Oh, *please* why doesn't someone help us to get down from here?" Miss Spider called out. "It's making me giddy."

"This could be a trick!" said the Head of the Fire Department. "Don't anyone make a move until I say!"

"They've probably got space guns!" muttered the Chief of Police.

"But we've *got* to do *something*!" the Head of the Fire Department announced grimly. "About five million people are standing down there on the streets watching us."

"Then why don't you put up a ladder?" the Chief of Police asked him. "I'll stand at the bottom and hold it steady for you while you go up and see what's happening."

"Thanks very much!" snapped the Head of the Fire Department.

Soon there were no less than *seven* large fantastic faces peering down over the side of the peach—the Centipede's, the Old-Green-Grasshopper's, Miss Spider's, the Earthworm's, the Ladybug's, the Silkworm's, and the Glowworm's. And a sort of panic was beginning to break out among the firemen and the policemen on the rooftop.

Then, all at once, the panic stopped and a great gasp of astonishment went up all around. For now, a small boy was seen to be standing up there beside the other crea-

tures. His hair was blowing in the wind, and he was laughing and waving and calling out, "Hello, everybody! Hello!"

For a few moments, the men below just stood and
stared and gaped. They simply couldn't believe their eyes.

"*Bless* my soul!" cried the Head of the Fire Department,
going red in the face. "It really is a little boy, isn't it?"

"Don't be frightened of us, please!" James called out.
"We are so glad to be here!"

"What about those others beside you?" shouted the

Chief of Police. "Are any of them dangerous?"

"Of course they're not dangerous!" James answered. "They're the nicest creatures in the world! Allow me to introduce them to you one by one and then I'm sure you will believe me.

"My friends, this is the Centipede, and let me
    make it known
He is so sweet and gentle that (although he's
    overgrown)
The Queen of Spain, again and again, has
    summoned him by phone
To baby-sit and sing and knit and be a
    chaperone
When nurse is off and all the royal children are
    all alone."
("Small wonder," said a Fireman, "they're no
    longer on the throne.")

"The Earthworm, on the other hand,"
Said James, beginning to expand,*

"Is great for digging up the land
And making old soils newer.
Moreover, you should understand
He would be absolutely grand
For digging subway tunnels and
For making you a sewer."
(The Earthworm blushed and beamed with
    pride.
Miss Spider clapped and cheered and cried,
"Could any words be truer?")

"And the Grasshopper, ladies and gents, is a
    boon
In millions and millions of ways.
You have only to ask him to give you a
    tune
And he plays and he plays and he plays.
As a toy for your children he's perfectly
    sweet;
There's nothing so good in the shops—

You've only to tickle the soles of his feet
And he hops and he hops and he hops."
("He can't be very fierce!" exclaimed
The Head of all the Cops.)

"And now without excuse
I'd like to introduce
This charming Glow-worm, lover of simplicity.
She is easy to install
On your ceiling or your wall,

And although this smacks a bit of eccentricity,
It's really rather clever
For thereafter you will never
You will NEVER NEVER NEVER
Have the slightest need for using electricity."
(At which, no less than fifty-two
Policemen cried, "If this is true
That creature'll get some fabulous publicity!")

"And here we have Miss Spider
With a mile of thread inside her
Who has personally requested me to say
That she's NEVER *met Miss Muffet*
On her charming little tuffet—
If she had she'd NOT *have frightened her away.*
Should her looks sometimes alarm you
Then I don't think it would harm you
To repeat at least a hundred times a day:
'I must NEVER *kill a spider*
I must only help and guide her

And invite her in the nursery to play."
(The Police all nodded slightly,
And the Firemen smiled politely,
And about a dozen people cried,
    "Hooray!")

"And here's my darling Ladybug, so beautiful,
    so kind,
My greatest comfort since this trip began.
She has four hundred children and she's left
    them all behind,
But they're coming on the next peach if they
    can."
(The Cops cried, "She's entrancing!"
All the Firemen started dancing,
And the crowds all started cheering to a man!)

"And now, the Silkworm," James went on,
"Whose silk will bear comparison
With all the greatest silks there are
In Rome and Philadelphia.
If you would search the whole world through

From Paraguay to Timbuctoo
I don't think you would find one bit
Of silk that could compare with it.
Even the shops in Singapore
Don't have the stuff. And what is more,
This Silkworm had, I'll have you know,
The honor, not so long ago,
To spin and weave and sew and press
The Queen of England's wedding dress.
And she's already made and sent
A waistcoat for your President."
("Well, good for her!" the Cops cried out,
And all at once a mighty shout
Went up around the Empire State,
"Let's get them down at once! Why WAIT?")

38

FIVE MINUTES LATER, they were all safely down, and James was excitedly telling his story to a group of flabbergasted officials.

And suddenly—everyone who had come over on the peach was a hero! They were all escorted to the steps of City Hall, where the Mayor of New York made a speech of welcome. And while he was doing this, one hundred steeplejacks, armed with ropes and ladders and pulleys, swarmed up to the top of the Empire State Building and lifted the giant peach off the spike and lowered it to the ground.

Then the Mayor shouted, "We must now have a ticker-tape parade for our wonderful visitors!"

And so a procession was formed, and in the leading car (which was an enormous open limousine) sat James and all his friends.

Next came the giant peach itself. Men with cranes and hooks had quickly hoisted it onto a very large truck and there it now sat, looking just as huge and proud and brave as ever. There was, of course, a bit of a hole in the bottom of it where the spike of the Empire State Building had gone in, but who cared about that—or indeed about the peach juice that was dripping out of it onto the street?

Behind the peach, skidding about all over the place in the peach juice, came the Mayor's limousine, and behind the Mayor's limousine came about twenty other limousines carrying all the important people of the City.

And the crowds went wild with excitement. They leaned out of the windows of the skyscrapers, cheering and yelling and screaming and clapping and throwing out bits of white paper and ticker-tape, and James and his friends stood up in their car and waved back at them as they went by.

Then a rather curious thing happened. The procession was moving slowly along Fifth Avenue when suddenly a little girl in a red dress ran out from the crowd and shouted, "Oh, James, James! Could I *please* have just a tiny taste of your marvelous peach?"

"Help yourself!" James shouted back. "Eat all you want! It won't keep forever, anyway!"

No sooner had he said this than about fifty other children exploded out of the crowd and came running onto the street.

"Can *we* have some, too?" they cried.

"Of course you can!" James answered. "Everyone can have some!"

The children jumped up onto the truck and swarmed like ants all over the giant peach, eating and eating to their hearts' content. And as the news of what was happening spread quickly from street to street, more and more boys and girls came running from all directions to join the feast. Soon, there was a trail of children a mile long chasing after the peach as it proceeded slowly up Fifth Avenue. Really, it was a fantastic sight. To some people it looked as though the Pied Piper of Hamelin had suddenly descended upon New York. And to James, who had never dreamed that there could be so many children

as this in the world, it was the most marvelous thing that had ever happened.

By the time the procession was over, the whole gigantic fruit had been completely eaten up, and only the big brown stone in the middle, licked clean and shiny by ten thousand eager little tongues, was left standing on the truck.

39

AND THUS THE JOURNEY ENDED. But the travelers lived on. Every one of them became rich and successful in the new country.

The Centipede was made Vice-President-in-Charge-of-Sales of a high-class firm of boot and shoe manufacturers.

The Earthworm, with his lovely pink skin, was employed by a company that made women's face creams to speak commercials on television.

The Silkworm and Miss Spider, after they had both been taught to make nylon thread instead of silk, set up a factory together and made ropes for tightrope walkers.

The Glow-worm became the light inside the torch on the Statue of Liberty, and thus saved a grateful City from having to pay a huge electricity bill every year.

The Old-Green-Grasshopper became a member of the New York Symphony Orchestra, where his playing was greatly admired.

The Ladybug, who had been haunted all her life by the fear that her house was on fire and her children all gone, married the Head of the Fire Department and lived happily ever after.

And as for the enormous peach stone—it was set up permanently in a place of honor in Central Park and became a famous monument. But it was not *only* a famous monument. It was also a famous house. And inside the famous house there lived a famous person—

JAMES HENRY TROTTER
himself.

And all you had to do any day of the week was to go and knock upon the door, and the door would always be opened to you, and you would always be asked to come inside and see the famous room where James had first met his friends. And sometimes, if you were very lucky, you would find the Old-Green-Grasshopper in there as well, resting peacefully in a chair before the fire, or perhaps it would be the Ladybug who had dropped in for a cup of tea and a gossip, or the Centipede to show off a new batch of particularly elegant boots that he had just acquired.

Every day of the week, hundreds and hundreds of children from far and near came pouring into the City to see the marvelous peach stone in the Park. And James Henry Trotter, who once, if you remember, had been the saddest and loneliest little boy that you could find, now had all the friends and playmates in the world. And because so

many of them were always begging him to tell and tell
again the story of his adventures on the peach, he
thought it would be nice if one day he sat down and
wrote a book.

So he did.

And *that* is what you have just finished reading.

AN INTERVIEW WITH
Roald Dahl

This interview, conducted by family friend Todd McCormack, took place in 1988, when Roald Dahl was 71. As Dahl himself said, "I have worked all my life in a small hut up in our orchard. It is a quiet private place and no one has been permitted to pry in there." He not only let Todd McCormack inside the hut, but also gave him rare insight into how he worked, where his ideas came from, and how he shaped them into unforgettable stories. Roald Dahl passed away in 1990, two years after the interview.

WHAT IS IT LIKE WRITING A BOOK?

When you're writing, it's rather like going on a very long walk, across valleys and mountains and things, and you get the first view of what you see and you write it down. Then you walk a bit further, maybe up onto the top of a hill, and you see something else. Then you write that and you go on like that, day after day, getting different views of the same landscape really. The highest mountain on the walk is obviously the end of the book, because it's got to be the best view of all, when everything comes together and you can look back and see that everything you've done all ties up. But it's a very, very long, slow process.

HOW DO YOU GET THE IDEAS FOR YOUR STORIES?

It starts always with a tiny little seed of an idea, a little germ, and that even doesn't come very easily. You can be mooching around for a year or so before you get a good one. When I do get a good one, mind you, I quickly write it down so that I won't forget it, because it disappears otherwise rather like a dream. But when I get it, I don't dash up here and start to write it. I'm very careful. I walk around it and look at it and sniff it and then see if I think it will go. Because once you start, you're embarked on a year's work and so it's a big decision.

HOW DID YOU GET THE IDEA FOR
JAMES AND THE GIANT PEACH?

I had a kind of fascination with the thought that an apple—there're a lot of apple trees around here, and fruit trees, and you can watch them through the summer getting bigger and bigger from a tiny little apple to bigger and bigger ones, and it seemed to me an obvious thought—what would happen if it didn't stop growing? Why should it stop growing at a certain size? And this appealed to me and I thought this was quite a nice little idea and [then I had to think] of which fruit I should take for my story. I thought apple, pear, plum, peach. Peach is rather nice, a lovely fruit. It's pretty and it's big and it's squishy and you can go into it and it's got a big seed in the middle that you can play with. And so the story started.

What is your work routine?

My work routine is very simple and it's always been so for the last 45 years. The great thing, of course, is never to work too long at a stretch, because after about two hours you are not at your highest peak of concentration, so you have to stop. Some writers choose certain times to write, others [choose] other times, and it suits me to start rather late. I start at 10 o'clock and I stop at 12. Always. However well I'm going, I will stay there until 12, even if I'm a bit stuck. You have to keep your bottom on the chair and stick it out. Otherwise, if you start getting in the habit of walking away, you'll never get it done.

How do you keep the momentum going when you are writing a novel?

One of the vital things for a writer who's writing a book, which is a lengthy project and is going to take about a year, is how to keep the momentum going. It is the same with a young person writing an essay. They have got to write four or five or six pages. But when you are writing it for a year, you go away and you have to come back. I never come back to a blank page; I always finish about halfway through. To be confronted with a blank page is not very nice. But Hemingway, a great American writer, taught me the finest trick when you are doing a long book, which is, he simply said in his own words, "When you are going good, stop writing." And that means that if everything's going well and you know exactly where the end of the chapter's going to go and you know just what the people are going to do, you don't go on writing and writing until you come to the end of it, because when you do, then you say, well, where am I going to go next? And you get up and you walk away and you don't want to come back because you don't know where you want to go. But if you stop when you are going good, as Hemingway said…then you know what you are going to say next. You make yourself stop, put your pencil down and everything, and you walk away. And you can't wait to get back because you know what you want to say next and that's lovely and you have to try and do that. Every time, every day all the way through the year. If you stop when you are stuck, then you are in trouble!

WHAT IS THE SECRET TO KEEPING
YOUR READERS ENTERTAINED?

My lucky thing is I laugh at exactly the same jokes that children laugh at and that's one reason I'm able to do it. I don't sit out here roaring with laughter, but you have wonderful inside jokes all the time and it's got to be exciting, it's got to be fast, it's got to have a good plot, but it's got to be funny. It's got to be funny. And each book I do is a different level of that. Oh, *The Witches* is quite different from *The BFG* or *James [and the Giant Peach]* or *Danny [the Champion of the World]*. The line between roaring with laughter and crying because it's a disaster is a very, very fine one. You see a chap slip on a banana skin in the street and you roar with laughter when he falls slap on his backside. If in doing so you suddenly see he's broken a leg, you very quickly stop laughing and it's not a joke anymore. I don't know, there's a fine line and you just have to try to find it.

HOW DO YOU CREATE INTERESTING CHARACTERS?

When you're writing a book, with people in it as opposed to animals, it is no good having people who are ordinary, because they are not going to interest your readers at all. Every writer in the world has to use the characters that have something interesting about them, and this is even more true in children's books. I find that the only way to make my characters *really* interesting to children is to exaggerate all their good or bad qualities, and so if a person is nasty or bad or cruel, you make them very nasty, very bad, very cruel. If they are ugly, you make them extremely ugly. That, I think, is fun and makes an impact.

HOW DO YOU INCLUDE HORRIFIC EVENTS WITHOUT SCARING YOUR READERS?

You never describe any horrors happening, you just say that they do happen. Children who got crunched up in Willy Wonka's chocolate machine were carried away and that was the end of it. When the parents screamed, "Where has he gone?" and Wonka said, "Well, he's gone to be made into fudge," that's where you laugh, because you don't see it happening, you don't hear the child screaming or anything like that ever, ever, ever.

How much has living in the countryside influenced you?

I wouldn't live anywhere else except in the country, here. And, of course, if you live in the country, your work is bound to be influenced by it in a lot of ways, not pure fantasy like Charlie with chocolate factories, witches, and BFG's, but the others that are influenced by everything around you. I suppose the one [book] that is most dependent purely on this countryside around here is *Danny the Champion of the World,* and I rather love that book. And when I was planning it, wondering where I was going to let Danny and his father live, all I had to do, I didn't realize it, all I had to do was look around my own garden and there it was.

Roald Dahl on the subject of chocolate:

In . . . seven years of this glorious and golden decade [the 1930s], all the great classic chocolates were invented: the Crunchie, the Whole Nut bar, the Mars bar, the Black Magic assortment, Tiffin, Caramello, Aero, Malteser, the Quality Street assortment, Kit Kat, Rolo, and Smarties. In music the equivalent would be the golden age when compositions by Bach and Mozart and Beethoven were given to us. In painting it was the equivalent of the Renaissance in Italian art and the advent of the Impressionists toward the end of the nineteenth century. In literature it was Tolstoy and Balzac and Dickens. I tell you, there has been nothing like it in the history of chocolate and there never will be.

Roald Dahl, born in 1916 in Wales, spent his childhood in England and later worked in Africa. When World War II broke out, he joined the Royal Air Force and became a fighter pilot. After a war injury, he moved to Washington, D.C., and there he began to write. His first short story was published by *The Saturday Evening Post,* and so began a long and distinguished career.

Roald Dahl became, quite simply, one of the best-loved children's book authors of all time. Although he passed away in 1990, his popularity and that of his many books—*Charlie and the Chocolate Factory, Charlie and the Great Glass Elevator, Danny the Champion of the World,* to name just a few—continues to grow.

Visit www.roalddahl.com to learn more about the author and his books.

✶ ✶ ✶

Quentin Blake has illustrated most of Roald Dahl's children's books as well as many others. The first Children's Laureate of the United Kingdom and a recipient of the Kate Greenaway Medal, Quentin Blake lives in London and teaches illustration at the Royal College of Art.